Dreams 1 - 2 - 3

REMEMBER, INTERPRET, AND
LIVE YOUR DREAMS

J. M. DEBORD

HAMPTON ROADS

Cover design by Jim Warner
Cover image: Midsummernight Dream, 2009 (digital collage),
    Skogrand, Trygve (Contemporary Artist) / Private Collection /
    The Bridgeman Art Library
Interior designed by Jane Hagaman

Hampton Roads Publishing Company, Inc.
Charlottesville, VA 22906
Distributed by Red Wheel/Weiser, LLC
www.redwheelweiser.com

Sign up for our newsletter and special offers by going to
www.redwheelweiser.com/newsletter.

ISBN: 978-1-57174-702-0
Library of Congress Cataloging-in-Publication Data:
DeBord, J. M.
  Dreams 1-2-3 : remember, interpret, and live your dreams / J.M. DeBord.
    pages cm
  Includes bibliographical references.
  ISBN 978-1-57174-702-0
  1. Dream interpretation. 2. Dreams. I. Title. II. Title: Dreams
one-two-three.
  BF1091.D34 2013
  154.6'3--dc23
                        2013026932

Printed on acid-free paper in the United States of America
VG

10 9 8 7 6 5 4 3 2 1

For my soul mate, Lisa, who made my dreams come true.

Contents

Acknowledgments   vii

Introduction   ix

Helpful Definitions   xv

Disclaimer   xvi

Part I. The 1-2-3 System for Living Your Dreams

Step 1: Remember Your Dreams   3

Keep a Dream Journal   8

Focus on the Three Key Elements: Symbols, Settings, and Characters   10

Look for the Three Narrative Components: Action, Reaction, and Resolution   45

Step 2: Interpret Your Dreams   58

Find the Threads: What Ties Everything in a Dream Together?   76

Mine the Metaphors, the Language of Dreams   79

Say the Words Aloud and Listen Carefully   84

How to Approach Nightmares   90

Recurring Dreams: Why We Have Them, How to Use Them   98

How to Know an Interpretation Is on Target   102

Step 3: Live Your Dreams   107

The Dream Oracle   112

Using Dreams for Personal Growth   117

Active Imagination   119

Inner Dialogue   125

Using Symbols   129

Part II: A User's Guide to Dream Symbolism

Archetypes	136
Body	142
Books	146
Children and Pregnancy	147
Colors	151
Death	159
Drugs	163
Flying and Falling	164
Former Partners	166
Marriage	168
Ocean and Water	170
Rape	172
Relationships	173
Sex	177
Shapes	182
Technology (Gizmos, Social Media)	187
Teeth	191
Video Games	193
Weapons	194

The Final Step: Putting It All Together 199

Conclusion 219

Bibliography 221

Acknowledgments

I am grateful to many caring and talented people for their contributions to this book. My partner Lisa not only shared her dreams but also her support during the years of work while I wrote and published it. My agent, Lisa Hagan, found the book the perfect home at Hampton Roads and provided the sort of guidance most writers wish they had. My editor at Hampton Roads, Caroline Pincus, deserves heaps of gratitude for polishing the manuscript, recognizing its potential, and turning it into a beautiful book. My mentor Larry Pesavento first taught me how to interpret my dreams. I would also like to acknowledge two users at Reddit, Alyssa Graybcal and Bob H. Howell. Alyssa volunteered her development editing services, and it was a real godsend because she saw ways to restructure the text and present the information better. Bob created the cover for the self-published version of this book after I dropped by Reddit asking for a favor. I am indebted to everyone involved and the Reddit Dreams community in general for their contributions. Thank you!

Introduction

Before the twentieth century, dream interpretation was a regular part of family, community, and spiritual life for many people. There was no shortage of dream interpreters because everyone, in a sense, is a dream interpreter. Then along came modern psychiatry, and dream interpretation largely disappeared from public view, obscured behind a wall of scientific jargon. These days, dream interpretation is dominated by specialists, psychologists, and gurus who took something that used to be freely available and installed a tollbooth. Now if you want to know what your dreams mean, you probably have to pay someone to tell you. And it ain't cheap.

This is a real shame, because dreams have the power to change lives. They can even play a part in determining the future. And they aren't that difficult to understand once you understand their language.

Dreams 1-2-3 teaches you my do-it-yourself process for interpreting dreams, knowledge that anyone can understand and apply. Experienced dream interpreters have learned a few things by reading this book, but it is written especially for people starting somewhere near the beginning. It is written for you. Welcome to the journey of a lifetime. It is going to change you in many positive ways.

I know that the knowledge in this book will change your life because it changed mine and the lives of the many people I have taught to work with their dreams. The very fact that I am writing these words is the result of a dream come true, in two senses of the word. One, I "dreamed" of writing a groundbreaking book and seeing it published, and here it is. And two, I had a dream that led me in a roundabout way to actually write it:

I am in a clothing store and decide to buy a jacket for work. The clerk rings up the sale and the price is everything I have in the bank. I forget the exact number, but I remember thinking, "that's all the money I have." I cancel the sale and lecture the clerk and a manager about their overpriced jackets.

Clues to the meaning of this dream are in plain sight once you know what to look for. A store is a place where decisions and choices are made. A jacket is a covering that says something about the wearer's profession, identity, and personality. A bank account is where resources are stored. So I interpreted the dream as meaning that the price of some decision I made about my work identity was too high, symbolized by the cost of the jacket matching my bank account balance. Next I connected that idea with my life.

A few days before the dream, I had started working in a new profession as a hotel manager in San Francisco. I thought it was going to be a terrific job, but after a few days of work my "dream" met reality: The hotel needed more help than I could give it. Working there meant draining my inner resources, symbolized in the dream as my bank account, to wrap myself in a new work identity as a hotel manager, symbolized by the jacket. A jacket covers, and in my dream the jacket I try to buy for work covers the real me, the author and dream interpreter. No wonder the price is so high! I had to admit what I already knew: Following my dreams meant writing this book instead of pouring my energy into a sinking organization.

I started writing *Dreams 1-2-3* the day I left the hotel for good, but really it was started twenty years ago when I first learned about interpreting dreams and how they change your life. Seeking help for how to live my dreams, in this case meaning achieve my goals and ambitions, I walked into the office of counselor Larry Pesavento, the author of *Toward Manhood: Into the Wilderness of the Soul.* Instead of repeating the same advice as everyone else about managing my time and being more disciplined, Larry asked me about my dream life. It seemed a little strange at first, but I'd heard somewhere that dreams have more meaning than we think, so I played along.

Larry showed me that the answers I sought could be found in my dreams, and my life changed in more ways than I can tell you. I gained insights, healed old wounds, broke old patterns, rethought priorities, trusted my feelings, and learned how to create the future I wanted. Now I am living my dreams, literally, and in the process achieving my most important goals and ambitions.

What Larry taught me is the sort of magic you want to bottle and sell—or write down and sell, like this book—but first I had to learn how to explain it. Dream work is a very personal process. You could have a dream identical to mine and it might mean something completely different to you than to me. There is no Rosetta stone for interpreting dreams, no universal meaning for every dream symbol, but there are ways of connecting dreams with your life and discovering what they mean to you, like I showed you with my dream about buying a jacket, and will continue to show you in the coming pages.

Dreams 1-2-3 breaks new ground by making dream interpretation understandable for everyone. You may find it different from other books about dreams in that it is neither scholarly nor New Age y. I assume you have no prior knowledge about dream work and take you step-by-step through the process, using vivid and informative examples gained from my work as a moderator at Reddit Dreams, a popular online dream forum, and two decades of personal study. We learn best by example, so instead of just telling you what you need to know, I show you through various dreams I have interpreted. With so many examples culled from people of all types, you are bound to run across some that remind you of your own dreams, and with the connection made you will begin to "get" your dreams. When that happens it's game on!

Learning to decipher your dreams is similar to mastering a foreign language. Dream language has nouns (characters and settings), verbs (the dream's actions and the dreamer's reactions), and adjectives (symbols and feelings experienced). At first only simple words and phrases are understood, then whole sentences and paragraphs, and finally subtext, humor, irony, slang. Eventually you will find that you not only understand the language but speak it fluently. Understanding dream language makes you a native within the borders of your sleeping mind, instead of a foreigner who doesn't comprehend the lingo. I will teach this to you.

In part I, I will teach you my three-step method to interpreting dreams. The first step is to *remember* your dreams and keep a dream journal. I give many tips and suggestions, so that even people who don't usually remember their dreams will learn how. I show how dreams are structured, how the structure gives clues to the meaning, and how dreams can be understood as cleverly told stories.

The second step is to *interpret* your dreams. I show you how anyone can do it by applying key facts and methods that uncover the meaning of the majority of dreams. For tougher nuts to crack, I share with you tools that can help pry open the meaning of even the most inscrutable or obscure dreams. Dream interpretation is not as hard as it may seem. It just takes practice, and you will get opportunities to practice what you've learned on your own dreams in the Make It Personal sections throughout the book.

The point of remembering and interpreting your dreams is to use what you learn to benefit your life, so in the third and final step I show you how to *live* your dreams, literally, by making them part of your daily life. Your dreams can solve problems, help make decisions, enhance creativity, discover or sharpen abilities, heal wounds, sort emotions and memories, run lifelike simulations to test you and spark personal growth, and even create the future at a quantum level.

To really make the most of it, your dream life doesn't end when you wake up; it continues throughout your day as you think about your dreams and work with them in your imagination. I will show you how it is done.

In part II, we will look at a great variety of subjects and themes that pop up in dreams, like flying, sex, love, colors, even Facebook and video games. Instead of trying to cover every possible interpretation and subject, I focus on how to decode the symbolism so that you can figure it out for yourself. And we conclude by applying what I show you to a number of fascinating and detailed dreams I have had the pleasure of interpreting. My hope is that by the end you will gain a good grasp for how to decipher the meaning of your dreams and use them for your benefit, and if I accomplish that, I have given you the greatest gift that has been given to me, other than the gift of life. This will change your life.

The life-changing part makes working with dreams so personally rewarding. My life has changed in great ways, sure, but even more rewarding is when I change someone else's life by offering my interpretations and advice at Reddit and elsewhere. It's pretty amazing that I can reach out from my computer and spread this knowledge around the globe, touching the lives of people I've never met. The responses and thanks I get encouraged me to go public with what I know. It made me realize the need for new voices to explain dreams. And the need for a book that explains dream interpretation simply enough so that anyone can understand it, but thoroughly enough that readers walk away enlightened to the meaning and intent of their dreams.

Read *Dreams 1-2-3* and you are well on your way to understanding your dreams. You will learn how to remember and journal them, learn the symbolism and symbolic language, learn to recognize the landscape and interpret the metaphors, and most important of all, learn to integrate them with your life. By doing so you address issues from your past and present. You create a better future. You know yourself and the people around you better than ever. And you discover a better person within you, able to live life to the fullest.

This is what it really means to live your dreams and make them come true. Before we dive deep into how to remember and journal your dreams, let's cover some helpful definitions first so we're all on the same page.

Helpful Definitions

The Unconscious

Throughout this book I refer to the unconscious side of the mind as the counterpart to consciousness. Everything is made of opposites, including your psyche, so the unconscious mind can be thought of as an opposite, or counterpart, to the conscious mind. It is the part of the mind that creates dreams; therefore it is an important concept for understanding them.

The unconscious, according to Jung, contains the memory of all human history. It is full of mysterious and fantastic images that cross cultural borders and appear in the dreams of people everywhere, and at root level it connects all minds together. Freud had a different idea. He saw the unconscious as a storage bin of infantile wishes and desires that extends no further than the individual.

I subscribe to Jung's conception of the unconscious, but simplify the idea in this book to mean the side of the mind that is separate from, but complementary to, the conscious side. I think of it as an objective viewpoint that differs from consciousness because it draws from a deeper well of memory and has no blind spots or ego turf to defend. The more you work with your dreams, the closer the two sides draw together. The ultimate goal is unity.

Be careful to avoid confusing *the* unconscious with being knocked out "unconscious" or sleeping "unconscious." In my early days of studying dream theory, the difference in meaning confused me. That is why I try as much as possible to use "unconscious side of the mind" or "unconscious mind" rather than just "unconscious."

The Subconscious

I also use the term "subconscious," and the difference between subconscious and unconscious can be hard to distinguish. Think of it this way: The subconscious is the middle zone between the conscious and unconscious sides. It is where information passes back and forth. Something that is just below your awareness is called "subconscious." If we compare this to baseball, we could say the subconscious is the on-deck circle, the place where batters get ready before taking their turn at the plate.

Ego

"Ego" is another term in dream work that is easily misunderstood. Many of us think of our ego as that thing that can be bruised. We associate ego with pride, stubbornness, or arrogance, but I use the word in its more psychological sense—to mean the part of yourself that you associate with your name. It is the main voice in your head, what people mean when they say "I." Ego describes an overarching structure of the psyche associated with personal identity and decision making. Dreams very often tell stories about the relationship between the ego and the rest of the mind, or between the ego and its environment: the people in it, the conditions and circumstances. In my opinion, most if not all dreams account in some way for the dreamer's ego.

Disclaimer

While dreams have been used in psychological therapy for more than a century, the advice offered in this book is from a layman's perspective, drawn from an ages-old tradition of community dream interpretation. The book explores psychological concepts and issues in relation to dreams, but is not offered to diagnose or treat mental disorders or psychological issues of any kind. Nor is it offered to treat or diagnose physical or emotional health. Dream work can bring about powerful changes in a person; please use it wisely.

PART I

The 1-2-3 System for Living Your Dreams

Remember Your Dreams

The first step in my dream work method is learning how to remember your dreams. Dreams can seem impossible to remember or not worth the effort, especially dark or painful ones, and this all-important initial step often seems the most difficult. But it's really not as hard as you might think. It just takes practice and a few good strategies. People also often think they "don't dream." I think it helps to know that, except in rare instances of brain damage, everyone dreams. Comatose people dream. Blind people dream. Babies in the womb dream. Even animals dream. If you think you don't dream, the truth is you simply don't remember your dreams. Don't worry. By the end of this chapter you will most certainly begin to. If you are someone who has no trouble remembering your dreams, you might want to skip ahead to the next section about keeping a dream journal (page 8). For the rest of you, read on.

In my experience, people's inability to remember dreams usually comes down to lack of time or desire. If you are too busy and distracted when you first wake up, your dreams will often slip away. But everyone who tries to remember his or her dreams eventually succeeds. Here are some suggestions for dream recall:

1. **Talk to yourself the night before.** Tell yourself before going to sleep that you will remember your dreams. Really *tell*

yourself. Say it like you mean it. Say it like a prayer. Anything repeated to oneself three times with full attention is likely to be remembered, so before going to sleep say three times, "I will remember my dreams." If you have difficulty saying it with conviction, you might be internally blocked—you say you want to remember but really don't, or don't think you can. If that's the case, relax and let it come naturally. By reading this book you are planting a seed in your subconscious, and once you know the true value and benefit of your dreams, you will wholeheartedly want to remember them, and the conviction to say so and mean it will grow.

2. **Write down your dreams.** Make time to remember and write down your dreams as soon as you wake up. This will require an adjustment if you normally start your day at a run, but it's essential. When I'm in a busy environment, I retreat to the bathroom with my journal first thing in the morning.

3. **Review at bedtime, cue your mind.** If you remember dreams from the last time you slept, review them at bedtime, or browse through your journal. By reviewing your dreams you cue your mind for that night's dreams.

4. **Don't move.** Stay in, or return to, the same physical position you were in when you first woke up. This physical cue helps jog dream memories and aid recall. I know someone who remembers his dreams as soon as he goes to bed, because the memories are stimulated by returning to a sleeping position.

5. **Meditate.** A clear mind, calmly aware of itself and its surroundings, is a great helper for remembering dreams. Don't let the word scare you. Meditation is any activity that holds your attention in a relaxed way, so a peaceful walk counts as long as you relax and clear your mind.

6. **Be patient.** The memories of your dreams are never lost, just stored away. There might be good reason why you block out some dream memories: They are too difficult to accept! Groundwork might have to be laid before the messages can be received. It's fine to be a turtle instead of a hare when it comes to dream work.

For most people, dream memories disappear soon after waking up, though the window of opportunity stays open longer with practice. So get in the habit of asking yourself as soon as you wake up, "What did I dream?" Hold other thoughts at bay as you look inside and ask that question. It's like staring into a dark night and waiting for forms to take shape. In that black inkiness are your dream memories. One memory, just a flash of a dream, is enough to give shape to the rest. Relax. Breathe deep. Search your memory. If a fragment of a dream comes to mind, ask yourself if it fits into a larger picture. For instance:

I wake from a dream and remember only that I was with my brother at a costume party. To remember the rest, I ask why we were there, how we got there, what we wore. I then recall that we drove to the party after visiting our mom. By asking why we visited her, I remember that we picked up costumes she made for us.

Once the initial association is made, it leads further into the dream memories. I usually don't need more prompting to remember the rest of the dream, but if I do I continue the same process of questioning the details and paying close attention to anything that compares or contrasts with waking life.

Waking up opens the memory hole and soon the details slip away, though you might remember other bits and pieces of a dream later in the day. By remaining at the edge of sleep longer and asking questions, the dreams aren't allowed to escape as quickly.

If you do forget a dream, don't fret: Dreams repeat themselves, displaying the same scenario a thousand different ways if necessary. In my experience, the dreaming mind is eager to get to work whenever I am, but the motor might take a few cranks to get started. If at first you don't succeed, keep trying.

If you draw a blank when you first wake up, pay close attention to your feelings, which can give clues to what you dreamed. Allow your imagination to fill in gaps; your intuition and feelings know what happened in a dream even if it can't be recalled. Also, flashes of dream memory can be remembered any time during the day. A simple act like sitting down to type at your computer or getting your usual cup of coffee in the break room can trigger a new detail of your dream to surface.

Don't judge a dream while remembering it. This can be a terrible hindrance by the ego to avoid painful or uncomfortable dream content. If the ego (see page xvi of the introduction for a refresher on how I use this term) is one-sided, dreams will go the other direction just as far to illustrate what is out of balance. In return, the ego, avoiding a hard look at itself, can go to great lengths to preserve its illusions. Everything seen in a dream is part of yourself or connected closely. Accept it. Embrace it. It's all you taking shape and telling a story about your life. Listen and learn; don't judge.

If you have tried self-suggestion and the other tools described here to remember your dreams and are still drawing a blank, try the following strategies.

Napping. No alarm to wake up to, no work day to begin. Napping on a sofa or guest bed can stimulate dream recall, as can any change of sleeping environment.

Going to bed at your regular time but waking fifteen minutes early to an alarm is another option. I don't like it because waking to an alarm tends to scatter my dream memories, but early sleep research discovered that people woken while having a dream are very likely to remember it.

Sleeping longer than normal is also known to help with dream recall. It gives the mind and body needed rest and opportunities to dream. People who go for long periods without sleep tend to have really bizarre dreams, which I attribute to rebellion in the unconscious side of the mind. Polyphasic sleep, sleeping multiple times in a twenty-four hour period, can also affect dreams. One particularly extreme form of polyphasic sleep known as the Uberman sleep schedule breaks sleep into six twenty-minute naps, one every four hours. This can produce terrifying dreams, according to some people who have tried it. You don't want to make an adversary of your unconscious mind; it needs complete sleep cycles of around ninety minutes to run processes for maintenance of mind and body, without which a person breaks down mentally and physically. Plus, with each consecutive dream cycle, dreams become longer and more meaningful. Half-hour naps don't cut it.

Some drugs inhibit dream memory. In my experience, drugs that aid sleep also affect dreams by making them strange and meaningless, or blocking memory. The small print is supposed to indicate if a drug affects sleep or dreaming. If you are taking a sleep aid, read the insert and ask your doctor about other methods of aiding sleep.

Going to bed intoxicated also affects dreaming, as does cannabis. Some war veterans use medical cannabis to escape the nightmares of being back in combat; like alcohol, it suppresses dream recall and interferes with the sleep cycle.

In recovery groups it is well known that soon after cleaning up from a drug or alcohol problem, a person will dream intensely. Dream activity usually picks up after a few days of sobriety, or after a few days of rest from a busy job. It gets intense because there is a backlog of dream content, but it's better to slog through and let the dreams run their course than use a drug or some other means to avoid them. I've also known people who have quit using tobacco or taking prescription drugs and began remembering unusually powerful dreams.

If all else fails, take a long vacation and leave the alarm clock at home. Extra sleep is the best stimulator I know of for remembering dreams.

Tip

If you wake up in the middle of the night and remember a dream, you only need to write down the major symbolism to jog your memory and fully remember it the next time you wake up.

Keep a Dream Journal

A dream journal will be your best friend when it comes to remembering dreams and should always be at your bedside when you sleep. Not only does it provide an invaluable record, but the act of writing is a physical cue that can aid dream recall by "getting in the flow." I use the same notebooks for making lists, jotting notes, and keeping track of dreams, but in my early years of dream work I used to have journals dedicated to just dreams. Your dreaming mind knows paper and pen are ready nearby as you sleep and will take the opportunity to give you something important to write down. Maybe not the first or second night, but the dreams will come. You only need one really "good" dream to get the ball rolling. In the meantime, journal as much as you can. Even fragments, impressions, and feelings are important. Use a voice recorder if pen and paper aren't handy, or a computer if that works best for you. I find that there's something about writing with pen and paper that helps me get in the flow, but it isn't really all that important what you record *with*. The important thing is to record.

Let me offer a few key pointers about writing down your dreams. Begin by noting the date. Note the characters from your dreams, the settings, the symbols, the time or time period, the actions that occur, your reactions, and anything that feels important or "clicks" in your head. Don't edit or censor yourself. Details that appear trivial or nonsensical at first can be important while interpreting later, so write it all while it's still fresh in your mind, including your thoughts and feelings about the dream.

1. Write your dream descriptions in the present tense. This is an important one. It helps to think of a dream as an active memory, a present situation described in the present tense. This makes it feel more immediate. So instead of "I drove to the store and bought some milk, and saw an old friend there," write, "I drive to the store and buy some milk, and see an old friend there." Present tense is a mental cue, a mind hack.

2. Now add a title to your dream. A title solidifies a dream in memory and provides a quick way of remembering it later. Titles also help track trends such as recurring scenarios, settings, and characters. If the point of the dream isn't clear at first, add the title once it does become clear. I recommend making up simple titles—a noun or two to describe the setting or characters and a verb to describe the action. Some dreams we'll look at later in this chapter have titles like "Plant a Tree with My Husband," "Walking the Platform," and "Swimming with Dolphins." Other titles like "The Snowstorm" and "Heavy Feet" summarize the dreams without using both a noun and a verb. You'll start to get a feel for this relatively quickly.

After accumulating several dreams in your journal, you will probably begin to notice patterns. Dreams run in cycles averaging roughly three months—this is the norm, not the rule. In my experience, when I'm feeling stuck in my life, my dreams will cycle around and keep coming back to the same point. When I'm making progress in my life, my dreams will spiral closer to the center. The door that was closed is open the next time it appears in a dream. The road that was blocked is clear. Try not to put too much pressure on your dream life, though. Some things take time and can't be hurried.

One circular dream pattern of mine involved flying to Paris. Something prevented me from reaching my destination, and my dreams told the story as a missing passport, a missed connection, a taxi that arrived late, or no money in my wallet to buy a ticket. Then my dreams took flight but didn't land. The cycle continued for several years until I understood what Paris meant to me and how to reach it in waking life. I'm working toward it by writing this book—Paris is, after all, a literary and intellectual center. It's also the city of romantic love, and I have that partner in my life now. No more dreams of trying to reach Par(ad)is(e).

That's about it for the basics of remembering dreams. Next we'll look at the basic elements found in most dreams. This information will help you identify the stories your dreams are telling. If you learn to think about your dreams as stories told through symbolism, sort of like parables, it helps you not only remember them but also interpret them, which we'll get to in Step 2.

Tip

Make your dream journal as detailed as you can. There is no such thing as "too much information" when writing down dreams.

Focus on the Three Key Elements: Symbolism, Settings, and Characters

I separate the three topics of symbolism, settings, and characters, but in fact they all belong under the umbrella of symbolism. I separate them because I think it helps you understand dream structure by learning to identify dream settings and characters as their own forms of symbolism.

Symbolism

Your education in understanding dreams begins with symbolism, because everything in dreams is symbolic, except on rare occasions when they speak literally. People are often relieved to find this out, because what compels them to seek my counsel is the fact that something very distressing is happening in their dreams: an evil shadow; a vision of murdering a spouse or harming a child. It's only natural that people would wonder if dreams like these mean that something is seriously wrong with them, and it can be a tremendous relief to discover that the disturbing dream is symbolic. The evil shadow symbolizes feelings about a threatening financial situation. Murdering a spouse symbolizes feelings of deep frustration with the person. Harming a child symbolizes feelings related to disciplining the dreamer's child.

When something happens in a dream that is outside the realm of possibility, like when you do something you wouldn't normally do, it's a clue to focus on symbolism. The next dream shows what I mean.

Pepper Spray

In my dream my four-year-old son is crying about something. Not acting totally obnoxious, just a little upset. I turn to him and spray him across the eyes with OC pepper spray. I see him clinch his little eyes shut and grimace; then I realize what happened and awake in terror. The dream stays on my mind all the time now. The fact that it was my hand that harmed him in the dream disturbs me so much I can't shake it. I can't figure out where the thought of spraying him came from; it is causing me a great deal of anguish.

This father would never spray his son with pepper spray in real life, so I immediately suspect that he does it in the dream knowing that the action is symbolic. My initial thought was that because his son is sprayed in the eyes by the pepper spray, maybe the dreamer might not be "seeing" something related to raising his child.

Next I focus on the pepper spray itself. The dream refers to a specific type of pepper spray—OC (oleoresin capsicum). The dreamer told me he had been sprayed with it while training for his job and said it's "like napalm on the face." He also said the use of it seemed "more punitive than anything else."

Now we were getting somewhere. The dream seemed related to the difference between discipline and punishment. The dreamer told me he plays the role of "bad cop" while his wife gets to be the "good cop" to their son, and he is tired of having to be the one "to bring the hammer down," to make his son comply after his wife tries and fails. The dream compels him to symbolically enact the meaning by doing something he would never "dream" of doing for real, as a way of dramatically expressing his feelings. The dreamer was relieved to find out his actions were entirely symbolic, not an expression of a hidden desire to harm his young son. A talk with his wife resolves the issue.

Tip

Dream images are generally not to be taken literally, but as symbols of parts of yourself and the dynamics of your inner life.

To get the gist for how dreams use symbolism, consider the following symbols that have popped up in dreams, and their interpretations. While the interpretations are based on personal experiences of the dreamers and therefore might not apply to your dreams, they are examples of how to think creatively when interpreting symbolism.

Someone dreams about going to his pantry and finding nothing but dog food on the shelves. This dream is telling a story about the dreamer's eating habits. He isn't really eating dog food, but his dreams tell him, because of his poor diet he might as well be. When dreams exaggerate or distort like that, the symbolism draws attention to itself.

A dreamer dreams of seeing her work supervisor get into a hot air balloon and float away. Does she really wish her supervisor would float away? Perhaps, but the balloon is more likely a symbol of how the dreamer subconsciously knows that the supervisor's "huffing and puffing" and verbal outbursts are only "hot air." It tells a story about her work life. Again, the symbolism is exaggerated and poignantly describes the situation.

One of my clients had a dream about a headless woman knocking over precious objects in her house. This symbolized how her fits of thoughtless anger were wrecking her family life. The headless woman tells a story about the dreamer, showing her behavior through the actions of a dream character.

A dream featuring a spoon showed the dreamer spoon-feeding a hungry mass of people. It tells a story about his life as a spiritual teacher who must "spoon-feed" lessons to his flock, lest he hit them with too much at once.

A fork in the road symbolizes a dreamer considering a job offer, a new path in life.

A missed carriage appeared in a dream by someone who had recently had a miscarriage, a sort of play on words (yes, really!). I'll explain more about this kind of symbolism in Step 2.

The meaning of a symbol depends on your personal experience and associations with it. For example, most native-born Americans see the Statue of Liberty as a symbol for freedom, but to an immigrant it might mean opportunity or inclusion. Foreigners might see it as a symbol for the United States and in turn what the US represents to them. A woman who dreams about a missed carriage but has never been pregnant might instead be viewing a story about a missed opportunity at romance, because in the Cinderella story Cinderella is taken to the ball in a carriage. Point is, the meaning of a dream symbol depends on you.

The difficulty with interpreting symbolism is that there are no universal symbols, no pat definitions that apply in every case. Therefore, instead of memorizing definitions of symbols, the best approach is to learn what your personal definitions are. It's not too hard because they are all based on your personal experience. Once you know what a symbol means to you, it becomes a tool for unlocking the meaning of the rest of a dream, like in *Wheel of Fortune* when one critical letter gives away the puzzle.

Continuing the game show analogy, symbolism sometimes reveals the meaning of a dream similar to how a *Jeopardy* answer reveals the question. Symbolism works backward in that sense, pointing to whatever root cause, issue, or question is behind the dream or a particular part of it. This dream from a female in high school shows what I mean.

Walking the Platform

I put on an orange sweater that is tight-fitting and ribbed. It is not a style I would normally wear. Then I walk in a line of my peers crossing over a dark pit on a narrow platform that can suddenly flip over. I see girls ahead of me fall off, but I manage to make it safely to the other side.

We'll get to the action of walking across a tricky platform and what that might symbolize in a minute, but first let's talk about the orange sweater. This is a gem of a symbol. The sweater is related to something "tried on," which can be anything new in life—in this case, I believe the sweater symbolizes a young person trying out sex. The color reinforces this interpretation, because orange is related to sexuality, reproduction, fertility (see page 153). Sexuality is new to the dreamer and feels confining, tight like the sweater. It's a "style" or lifestyle she normally wouldn't wear. So the question that answers what this dream means is, What activity commonly begun during teenage years is comparable to wearing a tight-fitting, orange sweater and walking across a tricky platform that dumps some of the dreamer's female peers into a dark pit?

By the way, when the dreamer reaches the other side, she enters a room with a sign overhead that says Prom. All she finds is a picked-over buffet and some bored peers. Can you figure out what that symbolizes? (Hint: It's related to the difference between expectation and reality.)

If you don't see how I made the connections between the symbolism and the dreamer, give yourself time to catch on. There will be many more examples in the coming pages. It takes experience and creativity to decode dream symbolism, but once you learn how you will never view your dreams the same way again!

Everything in a dream is metaphor, allusion, analogy, figure of speech, comparison—a representation of something else. To connect dream symbolism with yourself, look especially at the action of the dream. It's like the difference between a photo of a scene and a video of it. You have to guess at what is going on in a photo because the action is frozen in time, but a video shows it happening. A symbol by itself, just a photo, has a variety of interpretations. Combined with the action, it tells a story. Your dreams are stories about your life, so to understand what they are saying, start with the action.

For example, if you dream about a snake, ask yourself first what it is doing. Is it attacking you or harmlessly sunning itself? Is it wrapped around your neck or shedding its skin? Taken by itself, the symbolism of the snake has all sorts of possible meanings. The only meaning that counts, though, is what it means to you. A snake is a commonly known phallic symbol, but if a snake sheds its skin in a dream, the action speaks more to change or transformation than to sexuality, to shedding the old person and becoming someone new. It could relate to sexuality, but making an automatic assumption based on standard definitions takes the individual out of the equation, defeating the purpose of the dream. In the Action section of this chapter, I go into more detail about how action tells the story of a dream.

Knowledge of symbolism—not specific symbols but the whole realm of symbolism—is a dream interpreter's best friend, next to general knowledge about, and empathy for, people. Learning about symbolism is a natural way to expand your knowledge. The book *Man and His Symbols* by Carl Jung is a good place to start. In it, Jung shows the roots of common symbols, how they tie together across geographic and cultural lines, and how they are used by dreams to tell stories of deep significance for the dreamer.

Tip

A symbol is a shorthand way of expressing an idea. To interpret a symbol, ask what idea it expresses.

The next discussions about dream settings and characters are extensions of the symbolism discussion. The settings and characters are symbolic like everything else in your dreams. Learning to recognize the symbolism will help you with remembering and interpreting the stories.

Settings

The setting of a dream is also a kind of symbolism. Settings will often announce what area of life the dream is illustrating. It is one of the basic elements of any story. A dream set in a home improvement store, for example, might relate to improvements you are attempting in waking life, like getting in shape, eating better, or working harder. In which case, home improvement really means personal improvement. A gas station might relate to the energy that fuels your life, or the motivations that drive you to action, because a gas station is where you fill your vehicle with fuel. A library might relate to seeking or gaining information or knowledge, because a library is a place of information and knowledge.

The key to understanding what your dream settings symbolize is to ask yourself how they connect with you and your life. Settings that are exact duplicates from daily life might merely be helping to paint the scene for the dream to tell a story, but the majority of the time the settings are constructed from intimate details about your *inner* life, not your outer life. The settings are you, shown symbolically in three dimensions. They're snapshots of your interior landscape or situations you recently experienced, the movie set where scenes are played out related to your life.

As your dream journal thickens with entries, you will begin to recognize some settings because they tend to recur. And as you recognize the settings, you will make connections with your life: corresponding events, situations, feelings, or thoughts. It takes time, but with persistence you will figure it out.

Here is a setting from a dream of mine that explains what it is about:

I'm at my work desk, in the newspaper office, naked.

Dreams about work settings are usually related directly or indirectly to work. When I had that dream about being naked at my desk, my job as sports editor at a big college newspaper had just ended. Being the sports editor gave me a role of public importance that fit my background and personality. I wanted to go to the office and get to work, as my dream showed in the setting, but I didn't wear those clothes anymore. I was naked, in a sense. The symbols of nakedness and a former work setting indicate strongly that the dream is related to feeling naked without the job that defines my public persona.

In another dream, I am inside my house and am told that an angry man in the attic must be dealt with. I confront him aggressively, which doesn't help the situation. I figured out by working with the dream later that day that the attic symbolizes my thought processes, and the angry man is a part of myself trying to get my attention. The intruder was only hostile because I had been neglecting some basic needs, and deep inside I was angry with myself for doing it. (See page 120 for more about what the man in the attic represented.)

Houses

A life is said to be "constructed," and so is a body, so a house setting is a great way to symbolize your life or body. Dreaming about a place where you live is like a being shown the construction of your life in three dimensions from the perspective of the unconscious mind. Pay attention to details like the location of the house. For example, a dream set at a seashore can symbolize being at the border between the conscious and unconscious sides of the mind, where important information is coming through from the unconscious side. If the house is somewhere that differs from reality—like if you dream that your house is next to where you work or go to school, but in waking life you don't live anywhere near those places—the dream might be speaking to work or school life.

Because dreams like to "show" the meaning of the story instead of "telling" it, lower levels of a house tend to represent the dreamer's emotions, instincts, gut feelings, or hereditary roots—things which come from deep inside a person—while upper levels tend to represent the intellectual, mental, or spiritual life. Also pay attention to locations within the house for clues to the area of life being addressed. The front door, for instance, can symbolize the boundary between personal and public life, because the front door is often where visitors are greeted. It is literally the boundary between your private world inside the home and the public world outside of it. (See "Disappearing White Figure at the Front Door," page 206, for a dream that uses this symbolism.)

Kitchens, living rooms, bedrooms, and bathrooms are all used by dreams to tell stories. Kitchens are places where ingredients are combined together and cooked, and where food is stored and prepared. So a kitchen setting in a dream might relate to diet or anything that is "cooked up," like a scheme to make money, or a creation. Kitchens can even be used to describe pregnancy, since unborn children are called "buns in the oven" for good reason, or to describe how parts of a person combine together to form something new. Living rooms can symbolize living arrangements or the present state of your life. Bedrooms are used by dreams as a stage to act out feelings about related activities like sleep, sex, or pondering. In bathrooms we eliminate waste and work on our appearance. Occasionally dreams do something similar, cleaning up, confronting "dirty" subjects, or giving you a look in the mirror.

A house being invaded can be a sign that you feel invaded or violated in some way. Sometimes the invaders symbolize parts of yourself that want to "come in from the cold" and get attention, like the angry man in my attic. Other times the invaders are feelings, thoughts, or fears that aren't being consciously dealt with. The invaders could also represent people who don't respect boundaries or privacy, who "invade" your space. Ghosts in your house might symbolize fears or the things that haunt you, like regrets or a guilty conscience, or the feeling that you aren't really being noticed.

Cities

A city is another way of depicting your life, especially your public life, because cities are places of bustling activity where people go to "be seen" and public life is conducted. A city on fire might symbolize a life "going up in flames." A city flooded might symbolize overflowing or overwhelming emotions. A city being attacked might symbolize an attack on a person's reputation or lifestyle.

Airports, train terminals, bus stations, apartments, and hotels can represent transition, perhaps between jobs, living situations, points of view, or stages of life. Relationships also transition. In my dreams, the setting to tell the story of a changing relationship is an apartment or tent—but maybe your evolving relationship setting will be different. A friend going through changes in her relationship with her family dreamed frequently of being in transitional settings like hotels and airports with family members. To symbolize two friends going separate ways, a dream might show them catching different flights at the airport or boarding separate trains at the train station. Starting a new and exciting romantic relationship can be symbolized by taking off in a jet if that is what it feels like to you.

Cars

Vehicles like cars are another common dream setting. Dreams involving vehicles most likely reveal information about where you're going in life or where you want to be, and what is hindering or helping you along the way. They symbolize the way your life moves forward day-to-day (or doesn't). Vehicles can also symbol-ize the body, but this is less common.

For example, if you dream about driving a car that sputters up a hill, ask what is slowing you down or draining your energy. If the car slides all over the road, ask what part of your life is out of control. If you run out of gas or the brake pedal doesn't work, ask if something can't "get up to speed" or needs to slow down. If the wheels spin or the car goes in circles, ask what part of your life isn't getting traction, or if you're going in circles. If someone else is driving, look for areas where you're not making decisions for yourself, need guidance, or are "along for the ride." For instance, if your boss is in the driver's seat in your dreams and it aggravates you, you can bet that it's saying something about the relation-ship—maybe your boss has taken over the direction of your life! Then again, maybe the symbolism expresses the fact that your boss is the driving force behind your work life.

Vehicles are also settings that can describe group situations. I know of a dream about a flock of believers together in a bus driven by the pastor. The influence and teachings of the pastor provide direction in the spiritual lives of the flock, symbolized as the pastor driving the bus.

The Mall

Life involves making choices constantly, so a mall or store is a setting ripe with potential for telling stories about the choices we make. People "shop" for jobs, mates, lovers, and opportuni-ties. Also, the body and mind are in constant need of sustenance beyond nutrition, and dreams know where to find the resources. They go searching, shopping, while the conscious side of the mind sleeps.

In a dream about shopping for work clothes, the dreamer is considering a new job position ("The Maiden and the Matron," page 140). In my dream about buying a jacket that costs everything I have in the bank, the store setting tells me the dream is about making choices, and the jacket tells me it's related to my occupation. If you dream about shopping, think about decisions you have made, need to make, want to make, or that have been made for you. What choices are you presented with? What are the costs, and what do you get in return?

Restaurants

A restaurant is another dream setting that can speak to the choices and decisions you make. It can be used to tell stories about dietary choices, same as grocery stores and kitchens, but expand the idea of what can be consumed and you see the possibilities dreams have to work with. A restaurant could be a setting to illustrate how knowledge is consumed (see "The Fat Man and the Waitress," page 36). In another dream, it is a setting to finish cutting all emotional ties to an ex-boyfriend ("Cutting Ties with My Ex," page 167). If you dream of a restaurant, ask yourself about choices involving food or anything you "consume," like television programming, video games, sex, ideas, information, opinions, or knowledge, or about your recent choices in general.

Tip

When a dream setting differs from the real-life version, like when you dream about a house that is supposed to be yours but doesn't resemble it at all, or you go to work in a location you don't recognize, it's a tip-off to look for symbolism.

School

School is a dream setting familiar to everyone challenged to learn. After a day of learning something new, I sometimes dream of being in school. If I dream about a test I haven't studied for, it's often related to things I feel anxious about or unprepared for in my life. For example, while writing this book I had several dreams featuring school settings, and connected the dreams with anxiety about writing a book-length project. I had to learn as I go. The experience pushed me to master new skills.

School is also a social environment, and dreams can use the setting to speak about school-related relationships, self-image, identity, perceptions about society, or approval from adults and peers. If you dream of being in school, ask what you are being challenged to learn. Or ask if the school setting is connected with your identity or social relationships. If you are currently a student or work in a school, that setting in your dreams can speak to school or work endeavors, or to the relationships you have with the people there.

Bridges

Bridges can symbolize routes over an obstacle or from one place in life to another. Dreaming of standing on a bridge implies being between two places, like between phases or stages of life. I dreamt once that I was coming back from my mentor Larry's office. He worked in northern Kentucky at the time, while I lived on the other side of the Ohio River in Cincinnati, and my regular route home went over one of the bridges. Instead, in the dream I was confronted by a spaghetti mass of bridges and roadways, and I didn't know which route to take. My dream symbolized how I had gone through a process of dream work with Larry and it was time to "go home" and incorporate what I learned. I had a lot of different routes I could take, directions I could go in my life. I hadn't figured out yet where I was going, so I was on a bridge between what I had gained from Larry and what I would do with it.

Hospitals and Doctor's Offices

Hospitals and doctor's offices can symbolize healing processes of the body, but also of the mind, emotions, or personality. In my experience, these settings are just as likely to be used to tell stories about fixing something in the person as fixing something in the person's body.

The setting in the dream that follows helps explain the action that takes place there.

Killing Myself

I hang out in my friend's backyard with him and other friends, where I spend most of my time while awake. I can't stand it anymore, so I go to my mom's car and grab a gun from under the front passenger seat, stick it to my head, and pull the trigger. Everything goes black.

The setting reminds me of being a young man myself, hanging out with other young men with nothing to do except drink beer and talk big. The hollowness of that lifestyle grows in a bad way on the dreamer, who has this same dream several times. It tells him that his limited existence hanging out at his friend's house is killing him inside. It is a clue urging him to think about why he spends so much time there and what he'd rather be doing with himself. In this dream, his friend's house symbolizes feelings about wasted time.

He has "dreams" of accomplishing something, symbolized by his mom's car. Moms give their boys the ideas and inspirations that are built upon to become adult men. Growing up with a good mom is like riding in her passenger seat, which is where the gun is hidden in the dream. But her boy can only ride so far with her; he reaches an age when he has to make his own decisions and live his own life. If he doesn't know what he wants or how to get it, he feels ashamed of himself and worthless, leading to thoughts of suicide. The friend's house and the mom's car provide context for the action of this dream. They provide the framework for the story.

In the next dream we'll look at, the dreamer is a high school football player. The challenges of life can be compared to games. On the playing fields of the dream landscape, we learn about meeting challenges and developing potential.

Heavy Feet

I'm playing football and run for the end zone with the ball, but my feet are super heavy. I score and go to dunk the football over the goalpost, but it is higher than normal and I can't reach it.

In my experience, games are one way dreams that like to tell stories about effort. If the game in the dream is one you play during waking hours, the dream might have advice for how to improve. Athletes are known to dream about their sports and even foresee events that transpire. For example, legendary golfer Jack Nicklaus improved his swing and made history after taking his own advice from a dream.

The football field setting speaks to this dreamer's waking life efforts as an athlete, but also to his efforts to achieve goals in general. The dream is not showing him how to improve at football, but that something is holding him back or slowing him down, symbolized by his heavy feet.

Even though he scores, meaning he "gains ground" and achieves what he set out to do, he doesn't feel like he really attains his goals, symbolized by the goalpost crossbar set higher than normal. The dream says, in essence, that the dreamer's expectations are set too high, and it's a drag on his motivation. Dunking the ball through the goalpost is a touchdown celebration antic, and to be denied a celebration after "scoring" says to me that the dreamer lacks a real sense of achievement even though he is successful.

Symbolic meanings can change from dream to dream with the same dreamer, so further evidence is needed before reaching a conclusion about what a particular symbol means. A dream involving a roof can just as easily describe a thought process or perspective (as in "seeing the big picture") as it does a head. A basement can represent the bowels, but also a depository for unwanted emotions, among other things. Look closely at the action that happens in a dream setting before making conclusions.

Tip

To decipher what a setting means in your dream, ask yourself: What main activity happens there? How can it be used to describe something similar going on in my life?

Make It Personal

Go through your dream journal periodically and list out the settings. Take special note of recurring settings. Make columns with the settings on the left and your interpretations of the symbolism on the right. For settings with no apparent connections to yourself, think up possible connections and let time tell which, if any, are right.

Here are a few examples:

- Hospital = working on yourself, fixing something, healing

- Spaceship = mystery, exploration, cosmic experience

- Church = spiritual life, God, authority

- New home = new phase of life, new personal traits emerging

- Home improvement store = personal improvement

- Gas station = motivation, energy

- Amusement park = things done for amusement, humor

- Clothing store = persona, public image

Like with all dream symbolism, the meaning is often not clear at first. The very nature of dreaming is it reveals subconscious or unconscious information, so no wonder it is confusing at first! But somewhere deep inside you know what the symbolism means because it is based on your experience, and with patience and persistence you can figure it out.

Characters

People appear in your dreams intentionally. In some direct or indirect way, they are important to the story. I dream about people I know to find out about my perceptions of them, or to find out about parts of myself that relate to them personally. If I don't know the people in a dream, I first assume they are projections of my unconscious mind, parts of myself personified as dream characters, and are in my dreams to reflect myself back to me. A stranger might symbolize a thought, feeling, fear, character trait, or even structure of the psyche, such as the ego or an archetype.

Dreams with characters familiar from waking life tend to show how you process your interactions with those people, or how they influence you or make you feel. The underlying story might relate to the activities you do together, but more often it points inside you, instead of outside. Their presence in a dream can also be a way of conveying deeper impressions about the person, especially if you've had recent contact with them. I have dreamed about friends and relatives who were in situations that I could help with, as if the dreams were saying, "Hey, pay attention, this person needs you."

This next dream tells a story about the dreamer's interaction with a relative.

Missing His Shots

My uncle plays basketball and misses all his shots. Then he has shaggy body hair removed with large rectangles of sticky tape.

Ouch! Sounds painful. During the interpretation, the dreamer associates the uncle playing basketball with his attempts to "hit the mark" with arguments about politics and culture, but he misses his "shots." Asserting viewpoints is like a game to the uncle, and getting into debates with him is "sticky" in the sense that once engaged it is hard to get away.

The body hair torn off with tape represents the uncle's viewpoints, which are viewed by the dreamer as painful to bear. Since creatures covered in hair are perceived as primitive or instinctual, hair in dreams can represent instinctual behavior. In this dream, then, the removal of body hair might have a deeper message about the uncle's arguments going against nature or instinct.

Tip

Ask your dream characters for their names, either while dreaming or in your imagination afterward. This can help you identify what the characters symbolize if it's not obvious already. You can also give them names that seem appropriate, either specific names or generic titles related to the roles they play in the story, like "taxi driver" or "plumber." (For an example of how naming characters can be useful in dream interpretation, see the inner dialogue section on page 125.)

When you dream about people you know, a good question to begin with is, "what are the first things I think of in connection with this person?" Is she a great mom? Does he obsess about money? Do I admire her free-spiritedness?

Asking that question is how I helped interpret a dream about a guy who gives birth to a friend's baby (see page 149). It sounds strange until you think about pregnancy and birth as concepts that dreams can apply to a variety of situations. The dreamer describes his friend as hardworking and successful. The birthed baby, then, is the dream's way of illustrating that the dreamer "births" these qualities in himself because of the influence of his friend. If my friend Elmann, a martial arts master, is a character in my dreams, he most likely represents the part of myself that admires his discipline and skill.

We learn from the people in our lives and they show up as characters in our dreams, but those characters can also stand in for things we don't like or know about ourselves. A dream is a magic mirror that always reflects back the truth. Here is a dream that uses the dreamer's best friend as a character to show him a side of himself he is not fully aware of:

My best friend and I are in Las Vegas, partying on the Strip. We both have bottles of beer. For some reason, when we drink the beer it pours out the bottom of the bottles and into our mouths.

The phrase "bottom of the bottle" is enacted in this dream. It means drawn from the bottom of one's personality, character, or feelings. The friend is in the dream because their drinking behavior is similar: They both drink from "the bottom of the bottle," from their basest feelings and impulses, and the dreamer recognizes that part of himself in his friend, but not in himself. The friend is used as a mirror to show the dreamer a side of himself that is hard to accept for what it is.

Dreams will sometimes make connections between the characters and the dreamer. For example, on page 202 I discuss a dream about a guitar that turns into a child ("Playing Guitar in a Hotel Lobby"). The guitar and the child's shirt are the same hue of blue, indicating a connection between them. In another dream, a character chokes on a pill, which ends up in the dreamer's mouth. It is a play on the phrase "bitter pill to swallow," and the dream uses a surrogate to show the dreamer how she really feels. I find that people's dreams use surrogates to convey something that the person struggles with or consciously blocks out.

Another way dreams connect you with your dream characters is by showing the action from a character's point of view rather than yours. Seeing the action from another perspective gives you access to a side of yourself that isn't given as much attention or respect in daily life. For example:

An attorney who works for a cutthroat law firm dreams that there is a secret door in the building that leads to a drab, window-less room where a vaguely familiar man works alone chained to his desk. The lawyer sees through the eyes of the man as he goes about a typical day longing to be free, to breathe fresh air, sit in the sun, and do anything but work.

The character is tucked away in a secret room because he symbolizes a secret part of the dreamer that feels the same way, chained to his work responsibilities. However, to perform at his high-pressure job, he keeps the feelings secret even from himself. Though the attorney's office is lush in daily life, the drab setting of the dream symbolizes how he feels when he is there.

Characters can represent something about you, though with familiar characters the interplay of personal feelings, perceptions, and experiences are more complex. If the dream character is your father, for example, the dream probably illustrates something about his influence or your feelings about your relationship. But if the character is a father you don't recognize, the subject of the dream is more likely to be a look at fatherhood or something related generally. If strong emotions are involved, a "stand-in" character can substitute for the real person, so the dream can present the information without arousing strong emotions.

Accepting that dream characters are usually projections or representations of yourself can be difficult, but it's true. I remember getting a little freaked many years ago when a colleague told me she had dreamed I died. It bothered me enough to wonder if I was about to die. Now, after years of dream interpretation, I know what the dreamer saw was the "death" of a potential relationship with me. Our work relationship began with a romantic spark that never caught fire, and there came a point when the possibility passed without being acted on.

Tip

Expressions on the faces of dream characters often relate back to the feelings of the dreamer. If a character wears a happy face, ask yourself what you have to be happy about. If she is angry, ask yourself what you are angry about. If he is anxious, what are *you* anxious about?

Famous People

When famous people appear in your dreams, it's likely because some part of you relates to the role they play in society, or impressions you've gained from media exposure. If the person is an actor, the characters they play create perceptions that dreams use to tell stories.

To interpret why a famous person appears in your dreams, ask yourself what roles he or she has played, and think about your impressions. If nothing rings a bell, consider gossip you might have heard. If Charlie Sheen shows up in my dream with a big bag of cocaine, I know the impression comes from facts about his personal life!

For the next dreamer, a famous actor symbolizes a part of herself that relates to perceptions she has of him as a person.

Bad Tom's Pancake

I'm on the ground floor of a white multistory building with an open dining area and an elevator in the middle. Tom Cruise is near the elevator, and right away I feel something is wrong about him. Very persuasively he tells me to eat a pancake he has. Normally I love pancakes, but Tom is too insistent. I break open the pancake and show him it is raw in the middle.

In this dream Tom Cruise represents the side of the dreamer that is manipulative about food, an eating disorder personified around her impressions of Tom Cruise being cruel and persuasive. Cruise symbolizes the voice in her head that tells her everything will be better after she sticks her finger down her throat. He personifies the half-baked (like the pancake) idea that all you need is more willpower to overcome weakness, a notion that Cruise has pushed publicly in media interviews. Willpower certainly helps, but if a "weakness" is tied to survival instincts deeply ingrained from personal experience, no amount of willpower replaces the ability to care for oneself. The enclosed dining area in the dream symbolizes her stomach, and the elevator is her esophagus. Tom's location near the elevator is a clue that he is there judging every bite, which is how an eating disorder can work.

Another dreamer sees Napoleon order around people in business suits, and relates it to his authoritarian side as a supervisor at work. The dreamer gets results but drives relentlessly, showing his inner, tempestuous, general. By seeing this side of himself personified in the dream as Napoleon, he learns to curb his excesses.

Tip

Whatever qualities or behaviors your dream characters exhibit are probably true about you, too.

In another interesting example of how dreams use famous people as characters, a female dreams that Rachel Maddow, the television host and social crusader, asks on live television if the dreamer will marry her. The dreamer says yes to avoid embarrassing Rachel, then tells her after the show that she can't marry her. The dreamer relates the idea of marriage to other kinds of commitments, and realizes she had recently offered to lend her support to some social causes which she was unsure about.

In a memorable dream of mine, I met President Bill Clinton as he sat behind a desk. He stood to shake my hand. Suddenly a bunch of partygoers filled the room and crowded me out, and I recognized a bartender in the crowd who in waking life poured me stiff drinks. President Clinton represents the "presidential" side of myself that has a vision for my life and sets forces in motion to achieve it. The partygoers illustrate the main obstacle at the time: too much time wasted in crowded bars.

Casting a famous person in one's dream doesn't necessarily mean the dreamer is egotistical; it likely means that something about the famous person has resonated on a deeper level. If you have a raging need to be recognized, famous people can symbolize that need—after all, famous people in dreams are usually connected to you or your perceptions—but the same thinking applies to all dream characters. All of them are stand-ins, place holders for the psyche, actors playing roles. One thing is certain, though: Dreams pick their characters carefully. Nothing is left to chance. If you dream of a famous person, think about what you know about them and the roles they play; your perceptions of what they are like; and the talents, abilities, or characteristics you have in common.

Dream Pairs
Dreams use pairs of characters in a similar way to how they use famous people—to show a dynamic between you and something else—a part of yourself, a person you know, even between parts of your psyche.

Pairs are frequently presented by dreams as opposites, though the opposites are two sides of the same coin. One side of the pair will be old and the other young, or one male and the other female, one black and the other white, one aggressive and the other passive. It is an illustration of balance—or lack of it.

In my dream about meeting President Clinton, Clinton's opposite is the bartender in the crowd. While I had an inner Clinton representing my ability to lead my life like a president, I also had an inner bartender who had convinced me I could hold court on a barstool.

Here is part of a dream featuring a pairing:

I see a young stag and old stag. The old one is covered by battle scars. It attacks the younger one with its antlers. The younger one puts up a fight but is eventually defeated.

The pairing of the old and young stags and the action of battling each other symbolically illustrates the dreamer's relationship with her father. He is the old stag, a man quick to criticize and relentless in imposing his will. The dreamer, the young stag, is early college age and in the stage of life when questioning assumptions and authority is common. Her father has definite ideas for the adult he wants her to be, but so does she. Their ideas are very different, so the battles between them are epic. She puts up a good fight, but like an old boxer with tricks up his sleeve, her father breaks down her defenses. His method is symbolized by the antlers, with many sharp points sticking out all directions. His arguments are similar: sharp, and attacking from many angles.

The dreamer who saw Tom Cruise as a manipulative jerk ("Bad Tom's Pancake," page 31) had another dream featuring Gene Wilder. Wilder is a truly compassionate person, on screen and in person, which is how the dreamer needed to approach herself when dealing with her eating issues. Willpower wasn't the issue, as her inner Tom would have her believe. Approaching one life issue (her eating disorder) these two different ways (compassion versus willpower) was actually a deliberate pairing.

The core idea behind dream pairs is the "conflict of opposites." Sometimes the conflict is external, as in the case of the young dreamer and her domineering father. Sometimes it is internal, like the dreams comparing Tom Cruise to Gene Wilder. And sometimes pairing is symbolic of the psyche's dualistic structure. Strong leader and weak figurehead, genius and dunce, warrior and weakling, lover and hater—opposites can appear together in the same scene of the same dream, in different scenes of the same dream, or in separate but related dreams.

Carl Jung calls the process of rising above the conflict "transcendence," when the opposites unify above the conflict between positively charged and negatively charged internal energies that form the foundation of consciousness. This is done by recognizing the validity of both sides of a pairing and gaining a higher perspective.

It might seem contradictory to be both a lover and a hater, but opposites create dynamic energy, and it is up to the person to contain and channel it. What "hater" really means is detachment or indifference, as opposed to the lover's urge to connect. Too much connection leads to lack of boundaries. Too much detachment creates excessive boundaries. You need both to balance, not by expressing hate as well as love, but by realizing for every giver there is a receiver. Rise above the conflict to see from a third point of view that transcends, said Jung.

Similarly, it might seem better to be a genius than a dunce, but a genius amok is an arrogant little shit. Dunce can be a convenient label for the slower, more humble side of the mind needed to keep every genius grounded and open to information from all sources. In a series of dreams, a dreamer could fly but always hit an upper boundary and could fly no higher. I suggested that the dreamer was being told that the higher you fly, the deeper you must be grounded. Without roots firmly planted in the reality of here and now, he was limited in what he could achieve in his high-flying pursuits.

Here is a pairing from one of my own dreams.

The Fat Man and the Waitress

I'm in a restaurant sitting at a table next to a massively obese man eating a plate of spaghetti by rapidly sucking it down a noodle at a time. A waitress comes to the table, and I get the sense she is dimwitted. She speaks slowly and carefully. I become interested as she tells me about my past life. Somehow I know what she says is true, and I'm amazed that she has this incredible information. She says she tried once before to tell me about my past life, but I wasn't listening. She then tells me what my name was.

At that time in my life I was rather intrigued by the whole idea of reincarnation, the same soul living many human lifetimes. It went against my religious lessons of one life, one death, then Judgment, but I kept encountering evidence of its possibility in experiences reported by researchers, then in my dreams. The intellectual journey I was on at the time was exhilarating; however, I was becoming arrogant, separated from the world by knowledge few people understood, symbolized in the dream by the obese man devouring spaghetti. His inflated body was an apt representation of my inflated ego, and the noodles are like the information or "lines of thought" I consumed rapidly without chewing or digesting. What a pair we made! It took ten years for me to really accept that the dream showed me myself through that revolting character.

The role of a waitress is to deliver things, and in my dream she delivers information. She is the opposite of my inflated ego, with a simple job, simple appearance, and steady approach. Despite that, she knows something my oh-so-great intellect hardly grasped at the time. There are scriptures that say "God makes the most from the least," and "He who would be first should make himself last." Morality aside, the scriptures reveal a psychological truth, too: No matter how strong one side of a pairing is, it needs its other half to be complete.

Tip

Dreams pairs can have archetypal origins, meaning they arise from the fiery forge deep down in your psyche where consciousness originates. You will learn more about archetypes in Part II, "A User's Guide to Dream Symbolism."

Two Important Dream Characters:
Shadow, and Anima or Animus

There are two types of dream characters we have all met at one time or another. They are central actors in some of the most powerful, even life-changing dreams, and they are interrelated—your relationship with one affects your relationship with the other.

They are called shadow, and anima or animus, depending on the gender of the dreamer. They are your guides through dreamland, and your relationship with them determines whether you pass the tests presented by your dreams and advance, or you continue learning and trying. They are also two dream characters that affect your life directly: Shadow and anima/animus are active centers in the psyche regardless of whether you are awake or asleep. That means you have the opportunity to influence your dreaming life while awake, which you will learn to do in Step 3. The concepts were developed by Carl Jung and have withstood nearly a century of scientific scrutiny.

Shadow

If you do something out of character, such as forget an important meeting or inexplicably fall sick the day of a test you aren't prepared for, you can bet shadow is behind it. Shadow is why people sometimes sabotage their carefully constructed lives despite their best intentions, or do the wrong things despite knowing better. Shadow is the inner nemesis and must be handled carefully, because one's personal shadow connects with the collective shadow of all people, otherwise known as the dark side or evil, and the stakes are high when dealing with this part of yourself.

The easiest way to explain shadow is it's the parts of yourself you don't know about, the dark areas of your mind that could be conscious and under control of the ego, but are not. Though shadow can be personified in dreams as a distinct character, it has many personalities and takes many guises. Shadow's face in dreams is sometimes blurred, sometimes distinct. Its form is often black—black skin, clothes, or both—but also just "dark." I've encountered dreams of shadow represented also as Latino, Hispanic, Asian, Italian, Gypsy, Russian, even European-American—any group viewed by the dreamer as threatening. These associations are based on the stereotypes, fears, and perceptions of the dreamer, not on objective reality. Racial stereotypes are deeply embedded in many cultures and closely connected with the shadow side of our minds.

Shadow is why hubris leads to nemesis: The more the ego inflates, the more it blocks the light of personal awareness, and the more "shadow" there is for the inner nemesis to work in. The saying "the bigger the head, the bigger the shadow" expresses this idea. When the inflated ego doesn't get what it wants, it is prone to the opposite of inflation: depression.

Shadow can get you to work against yourself. In fact, it competes with you for control of your agenda. It is what makes you feel sick when you really aren't, because what you are "sick" of is not physical. I know someone who tripped and sprained her ankle on a morning when she didn't want to go to work. Guess what was going through her mind the moment she tripped? How much she wanted an excuse to take the day off from her demanding job! It can even influence outside actions and events against you, depending on how much power it is given. That is why I stress that it must be handled carefully.

Shadow is behind the characters that work against you in your dreams, symbolizing how you work against yourself. How do they (who are really you) do it? What buttons do they (you) push? What memories do they (you) bring up, or assumptions do they (you) make? What means are used to influence or control you? Anything you are angry or sore about is territory for shadow. Anything you might call a personal weakness is exploitable. Even people who rail on about politics, religion, or whatever are actually mad about something in themselves that they see in the "other." Otherwise, why care so much?

People who most strongly deny the existence of their shadow side are often the most strongly influenced by it. What you react to strongly in your dreams or in other people can be something you don't recognize or like in yourself, but your shadow sure recognizes it. Shadow is like the tour guide puffed up with self-importance by what it knows that you don't. Reverse that process, find out what your shadow knows that you don't, and you wrest back control.

Shadow is also made up of good or beneficial parts of yourself that are undeveloped or split off from the ego for some reason. Most parts of the psyche, in fact, have a shadow side (or the potential for it). Shadow isn't all bad; in fact, it's not really "bad" at all, just a function of the psyche like any other.

Ultimately, shadow is the test that prepares you for anima or animus work. It must be dealt with before deeper levels of the psyche are accessed, or else it poisons the relationship between the ego and the unconscious. Shadow is helpful for detecting bullshit, deception, and hypocrisy and unlocking creative potential, but first, you must sniff out the negative qualities. The more humble and aware you are, the more shadow becomes apparent, both in yourself and others—trust me, it's there whether you know it or not.

For an in-depth look at two dreams featuring shadow, see "Baby Draws Unbelievable Pictures," and "Getting Away with Murder at Laura's House," beginning on page 214.

Anima or Animus

Before beginning this discussion I want to stress that the concepts of anima and animus are based on traditional cultural norms, developed during an earlier era when gender roles were more strictly defined. Women were the masters of domestic life and men were the masters of commercial life. These days, gender roles are less clearly defined, but they still persist, with females generally taught to be sensitive and accommodating and subsume masculine parts of themselves in order to live up to feminine ideals. Males generally are taught to be aggressive and less sensitive, and to subsume feminine parts of themselves to live up to masculine ideals. Times are certainly changing, but these gender roles are not only ingrained in our culture, but in our psyches—and thus, our dreams as well.

Plenty of examples exist that turn these notions on their heads, however. The subject gets especially murky when gay, lesbian, and transgendered people are considered. But to understand how anima and animus work and what they represent, they are viewed through the lens of one's culture and its gender norms.

Anima and animus can be understood as the middleman (or middlewoman) between the ego and the unconscious mind. It is

called the "face of the soul" because it is the face of the unconscious mind. Anima, taking the form of an ideal woman, connects men to the deepest places within them. Anima's counter,
Animus, is the male face of a female's unconscious mind. Both
serve the same function: to spark personal development and
unify the conscious and unconscious sides of the mind.

Anima and animus are strongly attractive because they possess qualities of the opposite sex that are unconscious in you, but
can become conscious. These opposite-sex dream characters have
something you instinctively want and need to be a complete person. They can even act as templates for what you find most attractive in a mate, and help prepare you for meeting the right person.

When you meet her (anima) or him (animus) in your dreams,
you might think you have found the perfect mate, like in this
dream:

*There is this girl. The only way to describe her is simply per-
fect. Not Photoshopped model-perfect, but literally the girl of my
dreams. We hang out, carefree. It is summer and life is amazing.
Near the end of the dream we have to go to separate places. We
leave each other notes saying where we'll be. Weird thing is, by the
end I feel like I've known her forever. What does it mean?*

What it means is he met his anima in a dream! She is the
personification of everything feminine and unconscious in his
psyche. The male side of him is well-developed; he has been
taught all his life to identify with and develop his masculine
side, to be decisive, aggressive, and independent. But what about
a feminine side that is intuitive, nurturing, and cooperative? If
a man has the mistaken notion that he can't be sensitive and
also fully male, he will neglect his anima and dream of a woman
he wants more than any other but can't have. If he develops his
"feminine" side while still being fully masculine, he will achieve
balance and enjoy the benefits of being a strong, sensitive man.

Anima, then, can be described as a feminine sub-personality in men, and animus as a male sub-personality in women. Their purpose is to help you connect with traits of the opposite gender within you, lead you to deeper understanding and relatedness, discover what you are made of, and give meaning to life and inspiration for waging its struggles. Their ultimate purpose is to prepare your conscious mind for union, or marriage, with its unconscious side.

A man lacking connection with his anima dries up, feels listless, becomes a robot. If he has a bad relationship with his anima, he'll be moody, critical, and insensitive in his actions, but highly sensitive about how people act toward him. A good relationship with his anima will animate his life and make him feel like he is walking on air, crackling with creative energy. But if he overly identifies with his anima, he'll be too sensitive, a mama's boy. His dreams will tell him what the relationship is like.

A woman lacking good connection with her animus—her "interior man"—feels like life has no meaning, that she has nothing solid to stand on. If she has a bad relationship with her animus she is temperamental, critical, sarcastic. A good relationship balances her masculine and feminine qualities and makes her a force to be reckoned with, caring but firm in her values and beliefs. But if she overly identifies with her animus, she becomes rigid and judgmental, sometimes domineering and aggressive. Her dreams will tell her what the relationship is like.

Anima and animus figures in dreams are representations cobbled together from your life experience. Their faces are masks, so when looking for someone in the waking world innately attractive in the same way as this powerfully attractive dream character, or when searching your dreams for their presence, go by what you feel, not what you see.

Here is the dream of a woman who had a wild night with her animus:

I'm at a crowded dance club and make my way to the DJ. I ask him to play me something, and he puts on a slow song that's really cool, but the other dancers complain about the tempo. He and I ignore them and dance together. The night goes on and we continue to dance to the slow music. We kiss. I feel very attracted to him.

Be careful to avoid confusing a dream lover for animus or anima; they are not one in the same. The anima/animus relationship is usually chaste. A sexual relationship can be hinted at, such as in the slow dance and kissing, but usually not acted out because it creates confusion between the inner and outer worlds. (I know of quite a few exceptions, dreams of making love in a dream with an anima or animus figure, so really it depends on the person.)

A man can find a woman who embodies the sensitive, nurturing, and inspiring traits of his "interior woman," but he is asking for trouble if he projects those expectations of perfection. The bubble is bound to burst someday when fantasy meets reality. Similarly, a woman can find a man whose rational thinking, values, and independence are highly developed like her animus, but she is setting herself up for disappointment when his logic diverges from hers. Her animus is there to lead her to higher and deeper awareness of what she believes and feels, and to greater independence.

We see the dynamic at work in the last dream when the DJ chooses a song for the dreamer that she wouldn't have chosen herself and she enjoys it, but the crowd complains about the slow tempo. Females are taught to be closely aware of social reactions and accommodate for group opinion in a way that males aren't, but in this dream the dreamer learns to "dance to her own music." Most men are born with this independence; most women have to learn it. And most women are born sensitive, but men in general struggle to some degree with learning how to be both male and sensitive.

✳✳✳

Working with anima/animus and shadow will reap rewards. Jung coined the terms and first explained the theories supporting their existence in the psyche. He said that shadow is a sort of key master and anima/animus is a gatekeeper. The key is self-knowledge, and the gate is access to your full potential. Talk about living your dreams!

Tip

You can personalize shadow characters and anima/animus characters by naming them, or allowing them to name themselves. Mythological or heroic names are often appropriate: the Trickster or Pan for shadow; Guinevere or the Virgin for anima; Sir Lancelot or Hercules for animus. The right name will resonate with you; it will *feel* right.

Make It Personal

You will be able to wrap your mind around your dreams better if you keep track of the characters. Many characters recur because they are people actively involved in your life, or they mean something personally to you. Others recur because they are parts of yourself, depicted the same way repeatedly or differently every time. You will recognize them by how they make you feel. Just as you tracked your dream settings, make a column with your dream characters on the left and your interpretations on the right. For characters you aren't sure about, takes guesses and let time tell. Once you identify some of the major characters, your dreams become easier to decipher. It helps if you think of them as people in their own right, because they truly have a life of their own deep in your mind.

Now let's look back and phrase the questions to ask yourself when remembering and recording your dreams:

- How does the dream use symbolism? Can the action be described symbolically? Does something happen in the dream that is exaggerated or outside the realm of possibility?

- What are the settings? What do they symbolize? Do you recognize the landscape?

- Who are the characters and what roles do they play? Do they feel connected to you or show you something about yourself? What do you associate with them personally or with the roles they play?

Look for the Three Narrative Components: Action, Reaction, Resolution

Next we cover the narrative components of a dream and show how they tell the story of your day-to-day life. This will provide a foundation for remembering and understanding dreams, like how knowing the premise of a TV show helps with remembering and understanding its episodes. The better you understand the basic structure of dreams, the easier they are to remember. Understanding the structure helps by providing markers for the rational mind, places to engage mentally with the story.

Fully formed dreams have three main components: action, reaction, and resolution.

Consider this dream scenario: *You are an adult but find yourself back in grade school, confronted by a bully from long ago. You say, "I don't have time for this crap" before leaving the scene.*

Action: You are confronted by an old foe.

Reaction: "I don't have time for this crap."

Resolution: You leave the scene.

This simplified example is based on a common dream scenario: the nemesis or opponent. If you were the kid who got clobbered by bullies and are faced with similar behavior as an adult, you might find yourself in a rage at your sarcastic but harmless coworker, or at the jaywalker who carelessly steps in front of your vehicle. Dreams replay old scenarios to give you opportunities to work through unresolved issues that might cause you to overreact so you can put the past behind you. The nemesis must be dealt with—better to do it in dreams. In the dream scenario of confrontation with a school bully, the resolution is to walk away instead of fight. Busy adults don't have time to get absorbed in those games, or the luxury of losing their cool.

Action

Focus first on the action of a dream. It tells the story. Think of it like the plot of a movie or TV show. You are an observer who watches a story play in your head; now recall and describe it. The action doesn't always make sense, so look for memories of anything unreal or surreal. Often, that is what makes dreams memorable. If you wake up thinking, "what the heck happened in that crazy dream?" it is a good sign you will remember. Dreams are sometimes absurd to get your attention. Otherwise, I think a lot of dream material gets filed away in the brain like memories of driving to work or standing in line.

The action breathes life into your dream symbols. It shows you what is happening and makes the story move. The action is often where I find the meaning of the dream, like in the dream "Walking the Platform," mentioned earlier on page 14. It starts off with the dreamer trying on an awkward orange sweater, symbolizing how she has started a sex life. To reach that conclusion, I looked closely at what happens next:

I walk in a line of my peers crossing over a dark pit on a narrow platform that can suddenly flip over. I see girls ahead of me fall off, but I manage to make it safely to the other side.

Since the girls walk in a line, I guess that the action describes something all girls the dreamer's age go through, perhaps a rite of passage. I play with the idea of "walking the plank" and it leads to an association with "taking the plunge," and taking the plunge often refers to becoming sexually active. Some girls make it through the trials to reach healthy adult sex lives. Other girls don't make it, symbolized in the dream as falling into a dark pit. Navigating the transition to becoming sexually active feels dangerous to this dreamer, threatened with the possibil ity of falling. One sexual adventure where she gets pregnant or catches a disease or ruins her reputation, and into the pit she goes. The analogy is made through the actions of walking, balancing, and falling. Combined with the symbolism of trying on the orange sweater, it tells a story about a young woman becoming sexually active.

Here is another dream with an emphasis on the action.

Swimming with Dolphins

I swim swiftly and easily in clear blue water. Dolphins play nearby. It's exhilarating!

Clear blue water represents clear, calm thoughts and feelings, and water is sometimes associated with thoughts and feelings. Dolphins are playful and intelligent creatures, symbolizing qualities of the dreamer that enable her personal development. The action of swimming ties the symbols together and reveals the dream's meaning. Skillfully swimming in water implies that she can go down within herself, into her thoughts and feelings, into her very being, and emerge as a more complete person—a process of personal development that is truly exhilarating!

So to remember the action of a dream, begin by asking what happened and why. Where did you go, what did you do? Was there a reason or purpose? Remembering the reason behind the action of a dream can jog memories of other scenes, like in the following dream.

Plant a Tree with My Husband

My husband says he wants to plant a tree, and I think it's a good idea. We then plant a tree in our front yard.

In this dream, the action of planting a tree symbolizes starting a family, because trees are ready-made metaphors for families, and dreams love to use metaphors, as we'll see in Step 2. Plus we call family lines "family trees. Also notice that the tree is planted in the front yard where the public can see it, symbolizing how getting pregnant and having a baby are usually public events involving family, friends, coworkers, and neighbors. The dream tells the dreamer that her husband is ready and gives her the opportunity to decide if she is too. At first she only recalls that her husband wants to plant a tree, and remembering that part connects her memory with the next scene where they plant it. Time for that couple to ditch the birth control!

Walking a plank, swimming with dolphins, and planting a tree are just a few of the endless ways dreams use action to communicate their meaning to us. As you read the dream descriptions in this book, pay close attention to the action and think of it as a plot. Are you going somewhere, doing something, talking with someone, thinking about something? How do those actions mirror or relate to your daily life? Look for the symbolism, knowing that pretty much everything in your dreams is symbolic.

Reaction

For every action there is a reaction, and in dreams your reaction reveals how you feel about the scenario presented, which can affect the course of the dream. In the dream about planting a tree, the dreamer reacts by doing it—starting a family sounds like a good idea to her. If she disagrees with starting a family, the dream might show her trying to convince her husband to adopt a dog instead. In the dream about walking the platform, the dreamer reacts by taking her chances despite the risk. She could have stood off to the side in the dream, which some of her peers chose to do in waking life by abstaining from sex, but she feels she is ready and makes it across. If she was having risky sex, she might react in the dream by falling off.

In the next dream, the dreamer's reaction reveals something about himself that prevents him from achieving his potential.

Elevator Ride with Noam Chomsky

Noam Chomsky [the scholar and social critic] takes me on an elevator that stops at floors to witness scenes of civil protest. He explains why the world is in such a terrible state, and he's right, but I forget what he said. He then says to wait for a moment because he has to do something. When he leaves the elevator, I push the button for the bottom floor. The door closes and the elevator plunges down. It drops fast and scares me, giving me a sinking feeling.

As I discuss this dream with the dreamer, it becomes clear that the Chomsky character symbolizes the dreamer's intellect learning to discern the intricacies of the world. The dreamer has potential to be a Chomsky-like thinker, which is why he relates to this famous person, but a willful side blocks his progress and prevents his new knowledge from sticking (he doesn't remember what Chomsky tells him). He is given an opportunity to do it right by waiting for Chomsky to return but instead reacts by sending the elevator to the bottom floor. The movement down can symbolize going down into the body, but it can also have a more metaphorical meaning of the bottom of yourself, the basement of your personality or being.

The scenario is a test to see if the dreamer is ready for more, a story about his ability to learn. The rapid plunge of the elevator symbolizes the sinking feeling that a person gets when he or she has reacted impulsively and wrongly, because regret and the feeling of riding a fast elevator are similarly felt in the body. You can have these insights for yourself by asking how your feelings and experiences in your dreams are similar to your waking life. In this dream, the question to ask is, when else have I had a feeling like the rapid plunge of an elevator?

Tip

Sometimes dreams use narrative devices, like the elevator in the last example, to tell the story. In this case, the elevator itself is less important than the action that happens within it.

Along a similar line, another dreamer sees himself at a psychic training center. An older male scientist leads the dreamer with a group of trainees through the training center, stopping first in the military application wing. The dreamer is fascinated by the experiments in remote viewing and telepathy, but the group moves on to a classroom to begin learning. Instead of staying with them, the dreamer sneaks back to the military wing. While he is gone, a commotion breaks out in the classroom. A belligerent student bludgeons the teacher to death.

The dreamer reacts to the scenario of a psychic training center by pursuing his own agenda instead of learning what he needs to know, a sure way of losing whatever "psychic" or special abilities a person might possess. By sneaking back to the military wing, he "kills" access to the teacher within himself who can show him how to reach his full potential; the belligerent student is actually a part of himself that ignores rules and limits, blocking his ability to learn. Psychic ability symbolizes the deeper senses of the mind that gather information without a direct source, through intuition or subconscious awareness or extrasensory perception, and they won't be abused for long before receding.

The reactions of these two dreamers in similar situations expose personal weaknesses. They aspire to develop themselves, as seen in the setting of a psychic training center and a guided tour led by a famous intellectual, and their dreams set up scenarios to help achieve those aspirations. The dreams say, "Yes, you can do it, but there is something holding you back." These dreams are, in a sense, simulations—like the holodeck on Star Trek, where characters create holographic simulations to test themselves. It's a way of learning through your reactions, and reactions to the unexpected are most telling about who a person really is.

The dreamer in the psychic training center learns that his willful side interrupts the development of his mental gifts. In a similar scenario about learning to use one's gifts, the next dreamer's reaction prompts an unforgettable turn of events. He is a young boy when he dreams this.

God's Punishment

I play in my yard when God speaks to me from above. He tells me I can do anything I want, I can have the power to fly and make things appear with my mind. Everything is very bright and warm. At some point I come up with the idea of summoning a cloud of bees to attack people who have hurt me. Only those people, no others.

As soon as the bees go out and start to hurt them, the sky darkens and I feel God's presence return. I am instantly chastened. The voice

says in a very deep tone that because of what I have done, all the pow-
ers given to me are stripped, and I will be left alone and out of His
presence. I am stricken by this. The dream ends with me kneeling
alone by myself in the cold and dark, down where the family dog
ordinarily does her business, feeling utterly abandoned.

God is taken as a fact of life in the dream world. It can be
interpreted as a projection of the dreamer's beliefs, a holodeck
scenario like no other, a "God archetype" deep in the psyche
that feels like a divine presence when accessed in dreams, or
actual spiritual contact. Either way, this dreamer is shown quite
graphically the consequence of his choice to abuse his gifts. His
reaction in the dream to send a swarm of bees after the people
who have hurt him shows that he has a lesson to learn about
revenge. Fortunately it is "only a dream"—a chance to learn.
The unconscious side of mind has unlimited creative potential, and it uses dreams as a training ground for its conscious
counterpart.

Sometimes the reaction of the dreamer is central to further
progress of the dream story. The dreamer's choices affect the outcome of a dream the same as a reader's choices affect the outcome
of the plot, along the lines of the Choose Your Own Adventure
series. Those choices continue further in determining the next
dreams. Dreams can pick up wherever they left off and progress,
or rewind and replay.

In this scene from a long dream, the dreamer reacts wisely,
and wise choices in the dream world lead to benefits in the waking world.

Flying in a Spaceship

I fly as a passenger in an alien ship and discover the means of control-
ling it. The direction of the ship is determined by the vote of everyone
in it. I want to cast a vote, but think better of it because I don't have

a personal stake, and it would be wrong to interfere with someone's earnest choice.

The unconscious mind notices when a dreamer makes good choices. Choosing to not interfere with the course of the alien ship will, in turn, free the dreamer from interference in his own life, giving him more room to make his own "earnest choices." What one does unto others will be done unto them, one way or another.

Every dream scenario is ultimately created by the choices of the dreamer—choices made while dreaming or awake.

Tip

Because we are usually less restrained in dreams than while awake, your reactions in your dreams might show you how you *wish* you could react under the circumstances, instead of how you *would* react.

Resolution

The action and reaction of a dream lay out a scenario, an issue, a problem, a situation, a simulation. Question is, what resolves it? The resolution of a dream almost always points to an area of life that needs attention or has the potential for growth. Quite often the resolution is only hinted at, but it is there in fully formed dreams.

The resolution can be difficult to remember, but if you can recall the action and reaction, you only have to dig a little deeper to recall the resolution. It can be found at any point in a dream but is often near the end. If you remember a dream but not its resolution, it might be up to you to figure out how to resolve it. Remember, each of us gets to take an active hand in resolving our dreams.

Resolution can be the hardest component of a dream to interpret, because it is only hinted at or just isn't there—we have to search for resolution once we're awake. Some dreams are part of a series that won't resolve until the end, or until the dreamer makes the right choices. Other dreams imply the resolution through the issues presented, questions asked, and aspects of the dreamer brought to life.

In the next example, the dreamer is working at a family bakery when a commotion breaks out in the lobby. Left to deal with it alone and feeling resentful, he is pulled away from the disruptive scene by a helpful dream character. Then:

I see a young boy wearing a baseball uniform near the front door. He wants to leave.

I pulled this excerpt from a long dream to show how it resolves. Working for the family business symbolizes the dreamer's family obligations, and dealing with a commotion alone symbolizes his role as peacemaker and caretaker. It is a role he no longer wants. His dream sends a helpful character to create some separation from the commotion, enough to notice the boy by the front door. The boy's desire to leave, his position by the front door, and the baseball uniform—a sport the dreamer once played to make himself happy—represents the dreamer's resolution.

While the resolution of a dream is sometimes found in the action or reaction, other times it is symbolic and comes in the form of a suggestion. The boy by the door is the dream's suggestion to leave the family business and pursue a more personal agenda; quit doing what makes everyone else happy, and do what makes him happy.

The resolution of this next dream was revealed in a follow-up dream a few nights later.

The Snowstorm

I struggle in a snowstorm. Buried in the snow is a round amulet made of gold and silver. I pick it up and put it in my pocket. A white horse stands nearby. I want to mount it, but a shadowy man pulls the horse away from me by the reins.

Finding a precious object in a bleak landscape represents new growth in the dreamer's life, I know from previous experience with round, precious objects in dreams and the dreamer's feelings about finding it. The amulet's round shape symbolizes its purpose: to help the dreamer become a well-rounded complete person, (see "Circles," page 185). Blocking her way is the man who pulls at the horse's reins. The horse symbolizes her ability to move her life forward, so the shadowy man is controlling the direction and movement of her life. He symbolizes the side of the dreamer that keeps her in depression. White horses in particular are commonly associated with something that comes to the rescue, so his action of pulling the horse away from the dreamer is symbolic of how that side of herself prevents her from escaping the depression. Analysis of the dream and the shadow figure enables the dreamer to find resolution a few nights later:

I find the horse in the snowstorm and mount it. The bad man is nearby and I have to hurry. I urge the horse to flee. We come upon a cliff, and a lake is far below us. I don't want him to catch up, so I jump with the horse off the cliff and into the water.

The dreamer needs time before taking on the side of herself represented by the shadowy man. Jumping off the cliff symbolizes her trust that the way forward in her life has been found in her dreams, but it requires a "leap of faith." Immersion in the water shows that this is a time of healing for her—time to get away from the influence of the shadow figure and go down within herself. The ultimate resolution is to find her way around the obstacles symbolized by the man—obstacles that originate within the dreamer.

The resolution of a dream is a call to action, whether that action occurs during the dream or after it. For example, an addict in recovery dreams that his future daughter visits and tells him if he relapses, he will die before she can be conceived, thus erasing the possibility of her existence. The dream can be interpreted as a projection of the dreamer's fears, a graphic warning arising from the unconscious mind's ability to predict the future based on present and past circumstances, a call to use the dreamer's creativity before it is gone, or real contact with someone in the next life. Whichever way you interpret it, this dream is a call to action for the dreamer to recover from his addictions and get on with living well, or else he will miss out on something very important. The resolution is worked out by heeding the message of the dream and making changes.

Here is a similar sort of dream with a call to action.

Daughter Kidnapped at Day Care

I'm at my daughter's day care center and a voice on the loudspeaker says that children are disappearing. The adults are too busy to notice. I check out the place and find a man kidnapping my daughter.

The call to action in this dream is obvious, but people don't always take their dreams seriously. The dreamer senses that something is wrong with the care of her daughter. The dream announces that it is going on in plain sight, but the adults are "too busy to notice." A later segment of the dream zeroes in on the dreamer's boyfriend as the source of trouble. For her daughter's benefit, the dreamer needs to resolve this dream by changing the day care situation.

Make It Personal

Can you think of a time when your dreams have called you to act? My dreams have told me when to start projects, quit something harmful, get more exercise, take a break, get in touch with someone, move, and change jobs. Sometimes I know because of a hunch or feeling that comes to me around the time of a dream, but sometimes dreams show the suggestions directly through the actions and symbolism.

Do any reactions from your dreams come to mind? My reactions are often the most memorable part of a dream. For example, I don't remember what happened before I felt the big flying bug land on my neck, but I remember what happened afterward: I woke up actually slapping myself on the neck!

Can you identify dreams that have offered resolutions? You often know because something inside you responds with a resounding "yes!"

Now that you understand what the action, reaction, and resolution of a dream are, you can identify each and better remember what happens in your dreams. And as your knowledge grows, so will your dream memories.

When remembering and writing down your dreams, ask yourself:

- What is the action of the dream, the plot of the story, the theme?

- What is your reaction? What does your reaction say about your feelings or how you tick? How do your reactions affect the dream?

- What is the resolution, the moral of the story, the lesson, the call to action?

Once everything is written down and the questions answered, the fun really begins. Dream interpretation is a lot like a game of charades, guessing at clues until getting it right, and we explore dream interpretation next.

Interpret Your Dreams

An aura of mystery surrounds dream interpretation, conjuring up images of mystics staring into crystal balls or psychoanalysts reading the minds of their patients. But the essence of dream interpretation is really quite simple and understandable. Anyone can do it—no special training required. In the last section, I taught you that dreams are stories with structure and symbolism. In this section, we build on that knowledge by learning some facts about dreams and techniques for interpreting them that dispel the mystery and make you your own dream interpreter.

Internal versus External Dreams

Dreams come in two basic flavors: internal or external.

Internal (or inner) dreams are subjective; they describe what is going on inside you. External (or outer) dreams are objective; they describe what is going on in your life. By knowing if a dream is talking about your inner life or outer life, you can figure out the best approach for interpreting it.

Dreams about inner life are interpreted mostly by comparing the symbolism and details with your feelings, thoughts, and perceptions. Outer life details can be involved in the dreams, but at heart they are stories about your inner life.

Dreams about outer life are interpreted by associating with the events of the previous day and your impressions of the people and situations you experienced. You compare your experiences with the symbolism and details and make connections. The two flavors often mix, but usually a dream addresses one or the other. Sometimes you will use both approaches for the same dream.

With this in mind, let's start with the top three things to know when interpreting your dreams.

Top Three Things to Know about Dreams

There are three key ideas to keep in mind as you're interpreting your dreams:

1. Think of dreams as stories about you told from an alternative viewpoint, your unconscious mind. The stories show you something about yourself or your life but usually don't say it directly, instead using pictures and hints like a game of charades.

2. In some dreams, what you see is what you get. Look for the obvious.

3. Dreams draw their material from the past day or two of your life, focusing first on anything that was missed consciously but registered subconsciously.

We'll cover each of these points in depth in this section, looking at specific dreams as examples.

Dreams Are Stories About You
from an Alternate Viewpoint
Dream interpretation begins with understanding that everything in a dream relates back to you, the dreamer. Generally, the characters are projections of yourself, but they can also be representations of people in your life. The settings represent areas

of your life or of yourself. The symbols are derived from your personal experience. Dreams bring to life details about you as stories told symbolically, details from your inner life or outer life. It's your job to decode the symbolism and tie together the clues. The next dream, related to the dreamer's external life, illustrates what I mean.

The Deadly Pageant

My family goes to a casino where my sister is competing in a pageant. We get separated, so I call the hotel room where we are staying. My sister answers and I can tell something is wrong with our father, so I go to the room and find him dead with a sheet pulled over his face. But then he sits up and tells stories about when he was a kid.

The story being told here is heavily based on the dreamer's waking life. He recently found out that his sister has been having sex with her boyfriend, which is against the family code of no sex before marriage. Knowing that the dream describes an external situation in his life clues me in to how to interpret it. His sister is not in the dream to represent a side of the dreamer or a quality about herself, but to represent her actual self, just as the other family members are standing in for their actual selves.

The casino setting implies that the dreamer thinks his sister is gambling with her family life by doing something she isn't supposed to. The pageant is related to the theme of marriage because both involve putting yourself on display in order to be chosen. And the hotel symbolizes that the sister's life is in transition.

The sheet pulled over their father's face is a way of saying that the dreamer doesn't think that she is countenancing their father's instructions. Maybe she can't face the consequences of what would happen if he found out. The way the dreamer sees it, by having sex before marriage, his sister is choosing to ignore what their father taught them, since a sheet pulled over something is a way of ignoring it or getting it out of sight.

The final detail suggests, however, that the situation might not be as potentially cataclysmic as the dreamer fears. When their father sits up and tells stories about when he was a kid, the dream pulls another secret from the dreamer's memory: He knows that despite what their father teaches his children, he had sex before marriage, too. It's something he did when he was a "kid," around the same age as the sister.

Dreams like this are triggered by external events and describe what is going on in the dreamer's family life. The characters present are symbolic of actual people in the dreamer's life, while other details are symbolic in different ways, like the casino setting being symbolic of gambling with potential consequences. The next dream is similarly related to the dreamer's external life.

Raped at a Gas Station

I'm at a gas station pumping gas and some creepy guy checks me out. He grabs me, takes me around the side of the building, and rapes me.

Assuming this is an internal dream, we might wonder what is "raping" the dreamer's energy or motivation, since a gas station is a setting symbolic of where we "fuel up" to make our lives "move." The man who rapes her could very well be something in the dreamer's self that is hindering her in some way. However, this dream stems from an incident that actually happened the day before; some creepy guy actually hit on her as she was pumping gas. The rape is symbolic of how this man made her feel: like her dignity was taken, or that she couldn't control some situations. The rapist character and the gas station are drawn from her real experiences, and the rape symbolically expresses her feelings in response.

In Some Dreams,
What You See Is What You Get

Sometimes the meaning of a dream is literal. You don't have to interpret hidden meaning, but instead recognize the obvious. This next dream shows what I mean.

Lost and Found

I look around my house for a bull whip I lost years ago and find it hidden on top of a ceiling tile. While I'm at it, I remember a lost video game and have a feeling I'll find it buried down in the couch cushions. Sure enough, that's where I find it.

Interpretations of the symbolism of a lost bull whip and video game can go in several directions, but always begin with the obvious. When the dreamer woke up he checked above his ceiling tiles and found the bull whip exactly where he dreamed it would be. Then he checked under his couch cushions and found the video game. My guess is the dreamer knew all along where the bull whip and video game were, but the memories were "lost" to his conscious mind. The dream reminded him of what he already knew.

Some dreams are highly symbolic, while others have literal meaning. Like when Joseph was told in a dream to take baby Jesus and Mary to Egypt and hide from King Herod. Not an everyday dream, but you get the idea: If Joseph sits around asking himself if the dream means something symbolic and misses the obvious message to get out of town, that's a problem! The dream does not show him an internal situation, but an external one.

Dreams Draw Their Material
from the Recent Past

Whether related internally or externally to your life, the subjects of your dreams are derived mainly from events of the previous day or two, and the first subjects likely to be turned into dreams are drawn from anything you didn't pay enough attention to, need to understand better, or missed consciously but registered subconsciously: the look in an employer's eye before a change of work situation; the unspoken needs of a spouse or child; the amorous thoughts of a schoolmate or coworker; the second thoughts about a big decision. If missed consciously, dreams amplify your subconscious perceptions, thoughts, and feelings to bring them to your attention. In general, the more dramatic the dream, the more there is a need to give attention to something.

Because we are bombarded with subliminal information in busy environments, much of it is lost to sensory overload. But the unconscious side of the mind registers everything. It tirelessly records as the conscious mind goes about its day, without missing a beat.

When the conscious mind gives way to sleep, sensory input shuts off and the unconscious mind can say, "Great, now that I have your full attention, this is everything you missed while you were busy." It runs through a list of material, such as the dreamer's feelings in response to what happened the previous day, solutions to problems or questions, and new possibilities that could open up—a few among many possibilities for dreams to illustrate.

The Top Two Tools for Interpreting Your Dreams

1. Use association to uncover the personal significance and connections behind your dreams.

2. Break down your dreams into their elements (symbolism, settings, characters) and components (actions, reactions, resolutions), and build up the interpretations using your associations.

When an interpretation is on target it triggers associations. Something "clicks" or "pops" with recognition inside you. It feels right. Therefore, dream interpretation is largely an intuitive process of association between the dream and the dreamer's life, using feelings as a guide, as in this dream of an internal situation.

Stuck in the Train Station

I'm at a train station and my ticket is for train #9. An announcer says it is delayed because of an accident involving a car. The other passengers waiting for the train seem to expect the delay, so I resign myself to wait with them despite my aggravation.

Train stations in dreams often symbolize times of transition, but why train #9, and what is the accident about?

Because numbers in dreams can relate to times of life, I would start by asking what was going on when the dreamer was nine years old: significant events, important people, schools attended, places lived. Let's say the dreamer remembers that her parents divorced when she was that age, and life "derailed" because of the trauma of separation. Now stronger emotions come up; a part of herself badly wants to move on, to transition, but in a sense she is stuck in the train station with the other passengers. The feeling of aggravation about the delay is actually how she feels about the long delay in her emotional life. Associations like these are the essence of dream interpretation. Of course, it is rarely so easy. But with practice, association becomes more natural, off the top of the head.

Association is simply the first thing that comes to mind in relation to something else, flowing naturally—there are no right or wrong answers—by questioning the dream's details. The process goes like this for the last dream:

- What are the first thoughts that come to mind in relation to a train station? What about trains in general?

- Since the number nine came up in the dream, what happened in your life at that age? Does the number have significance of any kind, such as the number of members in your immediate family, or an address?

- Does the setting remind you of places you know from waking life, or from previous dreams? How do you feel when in the train station? Do the people there remind you of anyone or anything?

- Can you fill in details that aren't pictured in the dream, like the accident that delays the train?

The first thought that comes to mind about the train station is it's a place where people wait to travel, and trains take us to new places. We know the number nine represents the dreamer's age when her parents divorced. How does she feel inside the train station? Aggravated. Delayed. Stuck. The surroundings have a familiar sadness, she remembers after asking herself how it feels to be there. What are the other characters doing? Resigned to waiting, as if they expect the delay, because the dreamer has been mired in that emotional place for a long time. When associating, she sees in her imagination that the accident causing the delay stems from a family car broken down on the train tracks, like how her family life stalled when her parents split.

With the picture clarified she can use the message of the dream to work through her feelings and finally move on. She can tell herself that she should have gotten over it already, something adults tell themselves about old traumas, but feelings won't budge until they have been embraced and understood. When dreams open old wounds, it means the dreamer is ready to heal, or at least work toward healing, whether she consciously knows it or not.

Here is another dream interpreted using association. It is related to the dreamer's outer life.

Car with No Keys

I climb a steep path up a mountainside and at the top is a convertible sports car. I hop in ready to drive away after the long climb, but the keys are missing.

Climbing a mountain in a dream is sometimes a metaphor for a hard task or big project. The bigger the mountain and harder the climb, the harder the task, generally. In this case the steep path represents the dreamer's journey through college. The car is what gives it away—the dreamer remembered her father once owned a hot sports car just like the one in the dream. For his sake she excelled in school, but no sports car waited at the end of her academic journey in the sense of having a "revved up" career.

The last example shows dream interpretation in action: Take the dream in its entirety, break it down, and build it back up again using the dreamer's associations. You see how the setting announces that the dream is about a long and difficult task. You see symbolism in the car, the mountain, and the missing keys. You see the action when the dreamer climbs the mountain. You see the reaction: The dreamer hops in the car like it is hers, ready to drive away, showing that she subconsciously knows it really is hers. You see the resolution implied: The dreamer needs to find her own keys. One character is present—the dreamer—and another is implied: her father. He doesn't have to be present in the dream to still play an important role.

While each part of the dream conveys important information, only when put back together can an interpretation be made. The meaning is found by looking at everything, including parts of the dream implied or associated, and asking how it all fits together.

To further illustrate this point, let's look at two more dreams with similar themes.

I am in line at a graduation ceremony to receive my diploma. The stage is really tall and I have to climb a long set of stairs with the other graduating students to get there. From this upper view I see my father in the audience, but not my mother.

The metaphor of climbing a mountain is similar to climbing a tall set of stairs to get on stage. The setting of a graduation ceremony shows that the dream is school and career-related, and that the path to getting to where the dreamer wants to go is in line with the other graduates—who all had to take many "steps" to reach the top and earn a diploma. Why did she pursue her course of study? For her father's sake more than her mother's, shown in how he is present at the ceremony but she isn't. In the original dream he is not present, but is associated with the sports car.

The theme continues in the next dream.

It is Christmas morning and my family is opening presents in the living room. When I look under the tree, I don't find any presents with my name. I wonder if Mom forgot to wrap mine.

Like a sports car with no keys, a similar symbol in this scenario is a Christmas tree with no presents. The missing presents are a symbol for the career that is supposed to follow after graduation—not because a degree automatically means a great job, but because the dreamer excelled in school and did everything she could to prepare. However, her personal interests align more closely with her mother, who is missing from the audience in the first dream. Not until after graduation did the dreamer discover she had worked so hard to prepare for a career she didn't want. What she really wants to do is pursue her love of art and design passed on from her mother. That is her present to herself.

By acknowledging the feelings brought up by the original dream and thinking about the implications of its interpretation, the dreamer finds a resolution by pursuing a different course of study and work that springs from interests shared with her mother, while applying the work ethic she learned from her father. It's the key to starting her car(eer), the present under her tree.

The clues to decoding a dream are often in plain sight. For example, let's say you dream that three men trap you in a dark alley. You know they are Mafia and you owe them money. The Mafia detail is important because Mafia organize in "families," and dreams play with word meanings. The dream could be about a family obligation that has been neglected, symbolized as owing money, and the guilty feelings "pay a little visit," symbolized as three Mafia guys.

Four Important Dream Facts

Now that you see how personally associating with the details of a dream leads to the interpretation, here are four important facts to know:

1. Feelings are often central to the meaning of a dream.

2. Conflict between the head and the heart is one of the most common underlying themes.

3. Dreams say what isn't being said while awake. They amplify the small voices in your head.

4. Dreams exaggerate.

Processing Feelings

Feelings are the roots of many, if not all, dreams. I think feelings can tell you more about your dreams than anything else. Sometimes I remember a dream and have no idea what it means, but I know how I felt in the dream and immediately after waking up. By connecting those feelings with my life, I resolve some dreams without needing to fully interpret them.

If feelings aren't being acknowledged or expressed while awake, they are almost certain to pop up while dreaming, often in unrecognized forms. The underlying cause of dreams about being chased, for example, is often ignored feelings. These dreams are distressing, and the only good way to resolve them is to face them and whatever is chasing you head on. Ghoulish or disfigured characters in dreams can represent unwanted, ignored, hurt, or caustic feelings, which will go to ever greater extremes until recognized and handled by the dreamer. On the other hand, helpful characters and allies also appear in dreams, bringing with them positive feelings, solutions to problems, and keys to unlocking inner doors.

Here are a few examples of feeling-related dreams:

- Dreams of flying can express feelings of a personal life soaring.

- Dreams involving sudden pleasurable rushes like a roller coaster can symbolize feelings of pleasure from sex or drugs.

- Dreams about an out of control vehicle can relate to feeling out of control in life.

- Dreams about having heavy legs or the inability to move can mean feeling stuck in place or hindered in your life's progress.

In the next dream we see feelings of conflict played out between two sides of the dreamer.

Ron Jeremy Tries to Steal My Computer

A sketchy guy who looks like Ron Jeremy, dressed in torn jeans and a Hawaiian shirt, appears at my home and says he has to pick up *"the thing." I ask what "thing," and he says my computer needs to be repaired. I tell him I didn't call anyone to get my new $1,000 computer repaired, and he says the computer called to get itself fixed. I almost allow him take the computer, but think to ask it if it called someone for repair. The computer, as if sentient, says no.*

I first ask myself what could be happening in the dreamer's life similar to a sketchy dude brazenly showing up to take his computer. Someone really could be trying to take something of value from him. The dream could be about an external situation. However, that did not appear to be the case, so we looked at the dreamer's internal life.

Sketchy dream characters like the famous porn actor Ron Jeremy are often illustrations of sketchy parts of the person. If a person lies or steals or cheats or whatever, it'll show up in dreams as characters that lie, steal, or cheat. Even bad habits can be symbolized as dream characters that work against us, or as bad situations that can't be stopped. Denial and personal blind spots prevent the person from really thinking about destructive behaviors, but the dreaming mind is well aware. However, the dreamer did not relate to the Jeremy character that way, nor have any personal associations beyond the obvious.

Central to this dream is the computer. What did it represent to the dreamer? Two possibilities immediately came to mind: A computer is (1) a tool for work and (2) a source of entertainment. The dreamer said both subjects had been on his mind. He isn't doing what he really wants to at work—work that involves using a computer all day—and he plays video games a lot on his computer.

Seen this way, the Ron Jeremy character is the dreamer's perception of himself as a slacker who would rather play video games than work. Slacker dude is the side of the dreamer that prefers leisure over work and "steals" time from the ego, because he feels guilty when he chooses play over work. The resolution is to find a more conscious approach to balancing work with play, in a sense repairing his feelings about how he uses his computer, and perhaps find a line of work he can put his heart into. I also had to wonder if viewing porn takes away from his productivity, since someone who resembles a porn actor shows up at his home in the dream, but I didn't ask.

When broken down and put back together with the help of the dreamer's associations, the dream becomes clear: It represents a battle between his head and heart, one of the most common underlying dream themes. His head knows all the reasons why his computer should be used for work; his heart wants to use it for play. On another level, he sees the conflict between what he is doing for a living and what he *wants* to be doing. He can allow himself some slack, some leisure time, as long the slacker side of himself doesn't take anything valuable from his life.

Resolving Conflict Between the Head and the Heart

Dreams try to solve conflicts between the head and heart, like in the last example, but the clues are usually subtle. I look for it in any dream of conflict, realizing that everything depicted says something about the dreamer, and nothing kicks up dust like battles between the head and heart. It's pretty obvious in this next dream.

Groundhog Day at Boot Camp

I find myself back at a military-style survival training course I took last summer. Then I wake up with relief thinking it was just a dream, only to find myself back at the training center—I'm still dreaming but don't know it. I remember how I never wanted to take the training course, but it is paid for already so I feel obligated to be there, then count the days until it is over. I just want to leave but can't.

The dreamer's head says he has to take the training course because it is paid for already; his heart says he doesn't want to. His head overrules with the money argument, and months later he dreams he is back in a place he dreads and can't get away. Why? To revisit the scenario and find a better solution for next time a similar situation arises. Whatever compelled this sensitive soul to do something he really didn't want to is bound to happen again if he doesn't learn to listen to his heart, too.

The dream within a dream is the mind's way of tricking the dreamer into staying asleep and dreaming. Dreams serve an essential function of facilitating communication between the unconscious and conscious sides of the mind, as well as mental and bodily housekeeping duties, and the dream within a dream is a clever way of keeping the dreamer asleep and engaged. It can also be a way of symbolizing that the dreamer felt stuck in a situation he couldn't escape, same as he couldn't wake up from the dream. Dreams can also incorporate sounds from the waking world, such as the TV or a loud car passing by, and the basic purpose is to keep you dreaming or warn you of danger.

Amplifying Your Gut Feelings

When something really needs to be said but isn't, dreams find a way of expressing it, often with vivid imagery.

Dr. King's Robotic Hand

I bring Dr. Martin Luther King back to life and make him a robotic hand. We go to a city center in a postapocalyptic America. Dr. King gives a speech to a crowd near a fountain flowing with clean water even though he is not allowed to be there because he's black. Then my store manager comes out and reads from the law that blacks aren't allowed at the fountain. He stirs up the crowd with chants of "you can't drink here!" Dr. King walks off, saddened, and I want to scream

at my manager about justice, but instead follow after Dr. King and
find him in the garden at my house. I'm so mad I can't speak, and
wake up feeling pissed off.

In classic stories of things brought to life, like Frankenstein and Dr. Jekyll, the creature is born of its creator. In this dream Dr. King is brought back to life to voice everything the dreamer can't say about his work situation—to speak about truth, justice, and equal rights.

The robotic hand of Dr. King symbolizes how the dreamer's thoughts about his work situation turn to actions in the dream, because that is what a hand essentially does. Think "open the door" and your hand reaches for the knob. Reach for a glass of water and it follows the thought of wanting a drink. Think to yourself, "I need to express what's wrong with my work situation but am so mad I can't speak," and your dream produces a surrogate with a robotic hand to express what is unsaid.

When the store manager appears and brings down the law on the dreamer and his creation, I gain a vivid picture of his work environment. Denying him the good waters flowing from the fountain represents the manager's treatment of the dreamer compared to "preferred" employees, and even shows how the manager discriminates: by decree, company policy, "reading from the law." The postapocalyptic setting symbolizes the aftermath of the harm the dreamer's work situation is doing to him.

The crowd symbolizes the dreamer's coworkers, people in the same boat as him. At first they listen to Dr. King—to the harangue that the dreamer wants to deliver against his work environment, but uses Dr. King instead—then they turn against him because he's black.

Black in this dream represents the bias shown for some employees over others, an injustice that makes the dreamer fuming mad about unequal treatment. He feels like his manager is treating him in a way comparable to how he perceives black people are mistreated because of their skin color.

His agitated feelings invade the place where he should have peace of mind, the garden. A garden is sometimes symbolic of the center within a person that is free of turmoil, a place for relaxation and contemplation, especially after a hard day at work. It shows he is bringing his troubled feelings about work home with him, and it's making him a wreck.

This dream, like most, is in essence a survey of the dreamer's interior landscape, a snapshot of the interplay of feelings that arose the day before the dream. It shows how he feels about what is happening in his life and how it affects him. The subject of the dream is related to the dreamer's external life, but what the dream shows is what it is doing to his internal life. In this case, he draws his associations from both areas, but mainly from his feelings.

Here is another dream that vividly illustrates the internal life of the dreamer and expresses her conflicted feelings. She is in high school.

Unwelcome Company

I go with my "friend"—someone I don't know—to the video store to buy a birthday present for my best friend in real life (she likes movies). Some annoying girl I've never met wants to join us, and I'm too nice to say no. The dream skips and I'm with these two friends and around ten other people trapped in a really small room. People start to panic. I look over at the annoying girl who is supposed to be my friend. Her eyes are missing and there is blood everywhere. No one notices but me. The girl then drinks champagne and throws it up. Everyone tries to get out of the way. They turn on her and beat her up.

Because the "friend" and the annoying girl are people the dreamer doesn't actually know, this dream is likely about the "price of friendship" in general and not about specific friendships.

In the opening scene the dreamer is buying a birthday present for a best friend, symbolizing how friendships come with responsibilities and the potential benefits and drawbacks of allowing another person close access to your personal life. When the dreamer allows the annoying "friend" to join her, I am reminded of social situations at that age and people trying to fit in and awkward and superficial relationships.

Being too nice to say no to the annoying girl tells me that the dreamer doesn't know how to set boundaries with people, causing her distress. She tolerates people in her real-life social circle despite how uncomfortable she feels around some of them. The dream illustrates these feelings in the scene of being trapped in a small room, a metaphor for feeling "boxed in." The missing, bloody eyes of the annoying girl symbolizes that the dreamer isn't "seeing" something, namely her lack of boundaries and claustrophobic feelings. The fact that only she sees the missing eyes tells me that her views are not shared by her friends. The blood shows inner conflict.

Throwing up champagne symbolizes there is something the dreamer can't "hold down" any longer. Friendship is supposed to be about enjoying each other's company, symbolized by the champagne, but throwing it up shows that this dreamer doesn't feel much enjoyment from her friendships. She shared during the interpretation that she is a tidy person who likes things done a certain way, and it causes friction in her relationships. She also shared that she feels like her friends aren't that interested in really being friends, so in a sense she has no real friends.

When the annoying girl gets beaten up at the end of the dream, I see it as symbolic for how the dreamer's feelings and sensibilities take a beating from her social life because she is too nice to set boundaries and demand that people in her social circle respect her way of doing things.

Exaggeration in Dreams

In these last several examples, the dreams exaggerate to make a point. The blood and missing eyes in the last dream are powerful images that are easily misunderstood if not viewed as exaggerations. No blood has actually spilled, but it's a way for dreams to symbolize internal conflict and wounding. In the Dr. King dream, civilization is not about to end, but the way the dreamer feels, when exaggerated, is comparable to an apocalypse. In the Ron Jeremy dream, no one is actually out to steal anything from the dreamer, but it's an exaggerated way of symbolizing the feeling that the dreamer is stealing from himself. In "Groundhog Day at Boot Camp," the dreamer is no longer at the camp, but the dream shows him stuck there as a way of making him replay the scenario and learn from it.

With the tips, knowledge, and methods I've shown you so far, you can interpret most dreams. You now know the basics. Next we get into more advanced ways of interpreting dreams.

Find the Threads: What Ties Everything in a Dream Together?

When interpreting a dream, I look for a thread that weaves the story together, similar to a theme in a movie or novel. In the movie *The Sixth Sense*, for example, the color red ties together scenes involving death. In the book *Adventures of Huckleberry Finn*, the thread is the Mississippi River, which ties together all of the major events. Story threads like the ones I'm about to show you are not common, but they are a tool in the box of the master storyteller, your dreaming mind.

Here is an example of a dream that uses interconnected symbolism—a story thread—to express complex ideas. The dreamer is a teenager. His siblings in the dream are a couple years younger than him.

Building Sand Castles

I build sand castles at the beach with my brother and sister. The day is beautiful and we enjoy our project. I look behind us and see a giant wave rise out of the ocean. It crashes into the shore. I get away, and so does my brother, who easily jumps to safety. When the wave recedes I discover that my sister is buried in the sand. I dig for her, but our parents tell me she is lost.

The symbol that unlocks this dream is the sand. First, the dreamer builds castles out of it with his siblings, and the act of building a castle or house is a symbol for building up one's life. It happens externally as we acquire the trappings of adulthood, and internally as our personality matures. This dreamer and his siblings are at the beginning of a long process. They are still "playing in the sand."

Then the dreamer's sister is buried in the sand, and in analyzing that part of the dream the rest made sense. The dream tells the dreamer, if the situation continues on its present course, the impending wave of adolescence will bury his sister in the same stuff she would otherwise build her life with. The three siblings are all going about the same process of "building castles," and they face the same wave of puberty that sweeps away childhood.

The boys seem to be equipped to handle it: In the dream they easily jump to safety. I could guess though that his sister isn't as prepared. In her parents I see a possible source of her trouble, because they tell the dreamer to stop digging for her. He loves his sister and wants to help her, but his parents seem to have given up. (I could almost hear the "you're never going to amount to anything" comments.) And if that is the case, the girl is really going to need her brother's help to "build up" her life!

Sand ties together everything in the dream; it is the thread that connects the actions to the symbolism. The beach setting is used because it's related to sand, but I also think it shows he is becoming more conscious. More of what was unconscious in him is becoming conscious as he matures. His world is getting more complex.

It's not often that I get a dream to interpret where a universal rite of passage like adolescence and a symbol like sand reveal the meaning. Many dreams are too fragmented for a thread to emerge, or it is just not there. Threads can, however, emerge pretty often through the course of several dreams, either in the same night or over time. Being familiar with your dream characters, settings, and symbols, and writing a detailed dream journal, will help you spot the recurring elements that tie your dreams together. My dreams have several threads that have recurred for years and are easy to recognize now that I've put in the effort to track and understand them.

The next dream also has a thread. Look for it as you read.

Driving an Overloaded Bus

I drive a bus and stop for passengers who all get on carrying fast food bags. The bus struggles to move forward as more passengers are added. Up ahead, the intersection is blocked by a road crew, and the intersection is near where I used to live as a child. I see kids riding bikes on the sidewalk. One of the road crew guys, who looks fit and trim like my older brother, holds up a hand-held stop sign when my bus gets to the intersection. He says the road has been repaved, and the bus is too heavy to drive across it.

Buses and other sorts of large, lumbering vehicles are sometimes symbolic of overweight bodies. A bus, however, can also symbolize a group task or "vehicle of transition" in the dreamer's life, like a new job or relationship. Combined with the fast food bags and the action of driving an overloaded bus, though, the meaning of the dream points directly at the dreamer's body weight. Several other symbols and symbolic actions reinforce this interpretation: the way the bus struggles as passengers are added; the weight requirement to pass through the intersection; the implied comparison with the dreamer's "fit and trim" brother symbolized by the road crew guy. Then there is the stop sign, which says "stop taking in so much junk food!"

The dream provides even more clues. One is the intersection where the bus stops in the dreamer's old neighborhood. Places where someone once lived appear in dreams to compare between then and now and connect the past with the present. This dream also does it with the kids riding bikes, a type of exercise he would enjoy because he enjoyed it as a kid. The repaved road shows that a new avenue can open in his life; but in order to take that road, he has to lose some weight.

The thread is the bus. It is a symbol that ties the story together.

One last thing to consider before moving on. Consider potential real-world ties to a symbol before interpreting a theme around it. Otherwise, you might see a story thread where there isn't one. For example, the dreamer who dreamed about driving a bus did not drive one for a living. But he could have, and the possibility has to be ruled out before other interpretations are considered.

Mine the Metaphors, the Language of Dreams

Dreams use symbols and metaphors to tell stories. For our purposes, a symbol is a *part* of the story, while a metaphor is often the *point* of the story. The lumbering bus in the last dream is a symbol for the dreamer's body and a metaphor for being overweight. Going back to the dream about Dr. King brought back to life to voice grievances and demand equal rights, we see a metaphor for the dreamer's work situation, as well as a symbol for how he feels: discriminated against. Dr. King with a robotic hand sums up what the dream is about in one picture, one metaphor.

Dreams freely use metaphors, puns, figures of speech, analogies, and comparisons, both in words and pictures.

Here is a dream that combines the picture language of dreams with a clever metaphor:

I serve eggs sunny side up to my mom, dad, and sister.

Dreams are often packed with quick yet significant scenes like this one. Taken by itself, the metaphor of serving eggs has many possible interpretations. It can symbolize fertility. In Eastern and Jewish traditions, among others, the egg symbolizes the soul. And anyone watching TV in the 1980s in America will remember the "this is your brain on drugs" commercial with the egg frying in a pan. But a couple details from the dreamer's life illustrate what the egg symbolizes here.

First of all, the dreamer never eats eggs sunny side up, being afraid of possible bacteria in uncooked egg yolk. The dream sends a message with this detail, indicating the discrepancy is intentional and the dream has nothing to do with eating eggs.

Second, the dreamer plays the role of optimist in her family; she takes on a "sunny" outlook and hides her true feelings. She noted the irony of "sunny side up" because she is actually the one who recognizes the underside of her family dynamic. She carries the family secrets and knows the dysfunction that can hide behind what appears to be normal suburban life.

In this case, like most, the action tells the story. It provides definition of the symbol. Eggs served sunny side up show the dreamer's true perceptions of how she interacts with her family. If she is a pessimist, the interpretation as well as the dream itself moves in another direction: Some yolks might get broken!

An important point to keep in mind is that a symbol or metaphor in one person's dream can have a completely different meaning when used in another person's dream. Dream interpretation requires contextualizing a symbol or metaphor with your life. Here is another dream with a metaphor at the heart of the story.

Awaken from a Coma

I am in a coma for a whole year. I finally awaken and return to my daily life, and for some reason it's great fun telling people I'm alive. I read Facebook conversations my friends had about me when they thought I was dead.

The metaphor is found in the first sentence: coma. People are described as comatose when they are "dead to the world" or unresponsive, and this dream compares malaise to being in a coma. The dreamer had been out of circulation for the past year and recently "woke up" from whatever had been deadening his spirit. He was never truly comatose, but the dream exaggerates to make a point. The condition of his life was like coma, and apparently other people who knew the dreamer thought so too—which he visualizes as Facebook conversations that describe him as dead. Time to live again!

On a side note, another way dreams sometimes express the idea of dead to the world is with the walking dead: zombies. It is a surprisingly frequent dream theme often related to living in a society of seemingly directionless, mindless, sometimes threatening people, or to feeling directionless.

Metaphors describe the big picture of a dream, while symbols fill it in. Some symbols, like crosses or circles, are easily made into metaphors. For example, a circle is a symbol of the complete person, and dreams featuring circles say something about the process of becoming complete. Metaphor uses the symbolism of a circle to tell more about the story, say, by showing a doorway in the middle of a circle that the dreamer walks through as a way of symbolizing stepping into a new, fuller stage of life.

This next dream snippet is loaded with possibilities for making metaphors:

I clean my running shoes.

Shoes are used in many sayings like "kick the dirt off your shoes." Some shoes are "too big to fill." In this dream, since the dream occurred just before Thanksgiving, cleaning running shoes probably means preparing for something coming up that will require a lot of energy for "running around." The dreamer could be subconsciously preparing for the holiday hustle. Thinking more literally, if running is a hobby for the dreamer, cleaning his shoes could symbolize getting ready to push forward with a more rigorous running routine. Dreams are often used for this sort of preparation. Still more meanings for running are running for election; running away; and being in the running for a position, award, or title. I'm not sure of the specific interpretation of this dream—the dreamer didn't provide feedback—but it is a great example of the many possibilities a metaphor can present.

You see how interpretation is a process of trial and error. I like to say it involves throwing a lot at the wall and seeing what sticks. With the running shoes dream, I would "run" through every symbol and metaphor for shoes I could think of, and focus on the cleaning part, since the action of a dream tells the story.

Make It Personal

The dreaming mind speaks with pictures and uses metaphors to communicate ideas. Turn your dreams over in your mind and look at them in different ways, asking yourself if they can be described with a metaphor. Try starting at the end and working backward to the beginning. Or view the dream from the perspective of other characters in it, and ask how they would describe it.

Now consider this example and look for metaphors and symbols.

I am a ram on a hill, and at the top is an older, powerful ram. I don't know why, but when we lock eyes, we run at each other full speed and hit so hard some of my teeth fall out.

I invented this scenario based on several dreams I have interpreted that use similar imagery. The phrase being enacted is "butting heads," and I show it as action and metaphor. The hill in the dream symbolizes authority—"king of the hill"—and the rams symbolize the dreamer and his father. The dreamer doesn't know why he and his father butt heads and "ram" into each other, but the competition for authority is older than civilization itself and hardwired in the brain. Locking eyes triggers the struggle because it presents a challenge to the ram in charge. Fathers recognize when their sons challenge them and have an instinct for meeting it head-on.

So the rams collide and the younger one loses some teeth. It is a metaphor for losing the battle with his father, losing prestige since getting teeth knocked out is literally "losing face," as in losing prestige or dignity. I was also thinking of the phrase "loose in the tooth" to describe heated exchanges. When angry and challenged, a son can say things he regrets later, I know from battles with my father, but losing teeth in a dream has another meaning as the words we say that are hurtful or "loose." Losing a battle with a father wounds the son's pride, knocks him down a peg, brings out the worst in him, and he might dream of losing some teeth.

To reach an interpretation, you can focus on the symbolism and metaphors—butting heads, king of the hill, loose in the tooth. Or, if you are the son in the dream, you can ask yourself how the dream action can be connected with something recent, like a battle of wills with your father or a conflict with another male authority figure. The meaning is seen in the metaphor and the action. Who else butts heads like fathers and sons? Insert "teacher" or "coach" for father and you see a variety of situations this dream can describe with just a small change to the scenario.

Say the Words Aloud and Listen Carefully

Back in the 1970s, psychologist Ann Faraday proposed that dreams play with words based on how they sound. For instance, a dream involving a mailroom can be related to males or men, since "mail" and "male" sound alike (see "Mafia Slave," page 84, for an example). In "Baby Draws Unbelievable Pictures" (page 213), the dreamer is told his "blood will reign," not "rain" as he initially thinks. A missed carriage in a dream symbolizes a pregnancy miscarriage. Faraday's nugget of insight about dreams became widely known, and a dream that plays with definitions of words based on how they sound was thereafter referred to as a "Faraday dream."

For example, a man dreams that he climbs up a tree to a high nest to retrieve a pair of gloves at the request of his wife. The day before the dream, he grudgingly unloaded a storage locker because his wife "volunteered" his time to one of her girlfriends. He does it despite feeling irritated because his wife rules the roost and he thinks it is better to go along with her than object. The gloves symbolize the work he does, and the high nest is a pun for the word "highness," which expresses his feelings about how she treats him like a queen would a servant.

Faraday gives a personal example in her book *The Dream Game.* She spent the weekend with some people and their guest and dreamed about the guest dressed in a Nazi uniform. The same night, the guest dreamed about the rest of the group as participants in a play he was directing. Afterward, Faraday found out the guest was only there on a date with one of the women to get revenge on another woman. In other words, the charming, intelligent guest was "playing" them, just as he dreamed. And Faraday dreamed correctly of the guest depicted as a Nazi, an exaggerated way of showing his true nature as a person with no regard for others. Her dream picked up something hidden and made it obvious.

As I have applied Faraday's method of searching dreams for wordplay and puns, types of dreams that were once incomprehensible are now obvious in their meaning. Everyone can have dreams that manipulate language to give meaning and subtext. I suspect that the parts of the mind that generate language and the parts that generate dreams are closely related.

I run across dreams sometimes that seem impossible to understand. The dreamer has no associations, nothing from recent life can compare to the dream, no metaphor or wordplay is found. Some dreams are visualizations of bodily or mental background processes and have no larger meaning. But in my experience, most dreams—especially the most memorable ones—are meaningful to the life of the dreamer, and there is a technique for getting at it when all else fails. Once you get used to working with your dreams this way, you might do it all the time, instead of as a last resort.

It's simple: Picture yourself as the puzzling part of your dream, and talk from its perspective, whether it's a character, setting, or symbol. This example is borrowed from Ann Faraday and adapted for our use.

Say you are an adult woman who dreams of a puzzling setting, an open field, just a bunch of soil and grass, and you look down to see your jeans need to be repaired. The next morning you think back over the last day or two and find nothing in your memory related to fields or jeans. You think about possible interpretations for the symbolism and nothing rings a bell. You check your jeans for holes and there aren't any.

Begin by asking yourself, "If I am an open field in my dream, what do I symbolize?" Start talking like you are the open field. "I'm an open field and I'm in the dream because . . ." Well, you are an adult woman with a husband and no children, so you finish the sentence, "I'm waiting to be planted."

Now you have an association to work with—pregnancy; starting a family—and you look for confirmation by asking yourself, "I'm a pair of jeans in my dream and I need repair because . . ." The dreamer could be putting off the changes to her body from pregnancy, afraid she won't fit into her jeans, but the association doesn't resonate. However, she remembers a thought about her family history of disease that crossed her mind just before falling asleep, and she realizes she put off getting pregnant because she is afraid of passing on bad "genes," as in DNA. The jeans actually symbolize genes, and with that association the dreamer addresses a subconscious fear she will pass on a genetic disease to her offspring. It clears the way for her to feel confident about getting pregnant. The dreamer Faraday refers to got pregnant a few weeks after having the dream.

Tip

Gestalt therapy views everything in a dream as symbolism that the dreamer can potentially interact with while consciously using therapeutic techniques. If you are interested in learning more about interpreting dreams using Gestalt therapy, you can read Faraday's books and look up Fritz Perls, the founder of Gestalt therapy.

Even using all the tools in the interpreter's box that I've shown you so far, there are still dreams that resist all attempts at interpretation. The next dream was one such case. It opened my eyes to a new way of understanding how and why dreams tell their stories, and the clever ways they do it.

WARNING: The Following Dream Contains Graphic Language That May Be Upsetting to Some Readers

Perverted Boy Follows Me

There is a young boy age four or five who follows me as I go about my day, and only I can see and hear him. His face is blurred, but I see that he has huge orange eyes. I walk to class and he "floats" along beside me and says nasty stuff about people we pass on the sidewalk, like "That guy is a homo who wants to stick his dick in your ass." Then I'm with my girlfriend and my father, and the child says that my father secretly wants to bang my girlfriend. Later, I'm in my bedroom and hear my cousin in her bedroom next to mine (in waking life she lives with my family), and the child says that she's doing drugs and fucking some dude right now, and I should go fuck her too. Whenever the child speaks, it repeats itself and won't shut up until I look at it.

On first look, this dream seems to say that the dreamer has repressed or indulged something that manifests in his dream as a vile young boy. I suspect that he indulges thoughts similar to what the boy voices, maybe even watches too much bad TV, and perhaps some shadowy part of himself pops up as a result. Dreams are known to take small thoughts and exaggerate them as a way of making the dreamer aware of the danger of allowing the seed to take root. But I'm way off; the dreamer can't associate anything I suggest with his waking life. He wasn't molested as a child. He has no lurking fantasies about his cousin. So I ask him to think back on the day before the dream and connect it with the boy.

The dreamer remembers he had been studying child perversion in his psychology class, and his classmates shared some shocking personal stories. Now the dream starts to make sense. In it, the dreamer goes about an ordinary day, which includes going to class. It is a hint that the boy is somehow related to the class. Then I consider what the dreamer studies and realize that the dream illustrates it "beautifully."

The dream takes what the dreamer learns from the class material and the stories of his classmates and makes it real in an unforgettable way, a graphic portrayal of child perversion. I've known dreams to run through learning simulations as a way to make subjects less abstract and more concrete, but I had never seen it done like this. It's one thing to learn about child perversion by studying it; it's another to have a perverted child follow you around all day making the most revolting remarks!

The fact that the dream character repeats itself until the dreamer looks at it is telling, because the dreamer is also "looking at" the subject of child perversion in his waking life. It is a way of saying, "Do you *see* what I'm talking about?" The child's big orange eyes are a mystery. My guess is, since the dream is related to child perversion, and perversion is related to unhealthy sexuality, the orange color is a way of showing the sexual roots, and the eyes are a clue to really "see" it. It might have been part of the school lesson that he overlooked. The child's comments are sexual and derogatory, and sexual abuse is a big factor in child perversion.

While I have been stressing throughout this book that dreams have meaning, sometimes dream characters are only visualizations of internal processes, and the subsequent dreams have no more meaning than that. Most of the crew that run your internal machinery are "below deck," the deck being your conscious awareness. The processes of that machinery are often shown in dreams as characters performing work roles, though often the dreams are not remembered. I don't want to say that these dreams have no meaning, because anything you can learn about how you tick is meaningful, but there is not a lot to interpret that you need to know. This next dream illustrates what I mean.

Fish Eats Coffee from My Knee

I'm presented with a big, toothy fish and told that it needs to eat the coffee that has accumulated in my knee. I agree, and feel no pain when it latches on and feeds. When it's done I toss it into a pool with other brightly colored fish, and it eats some of them.

A fish eating coffee is a great analogy for antibodies that clean out or "eat" debris from the dreamer's knee, since fish swim in water and antibodies swim in the bloodstream. My interpretation reminds the dreamer that he has been hearing a funny sound in his knee. The dream compares the sound to the grinding of coffee beans.

The fish with the big teeth is the solution because it symbolizes the antibodies that travel through the bloodstream and clean out debris. Antibodies attack other parts of the body, too, and I think that is symbolized by the fish attacking other fish when it is done with the knee. What the dreamer witnesses is his body repairing itself while he sleeps. I interpreted the dream this way instead of using the symbolism of fish or knees, or considering what the action of biting can mean, because the dreamer easily agrees to let the fish feed off him and feels no pain. This tells me he subconsciously knows it is beneficial.

Tip

If you've tried the tips and techniques here and the meaning of your dream is still not clear, review the dream just before going to sleep and ask for clarification. Your unconscious mind wants you to know the meaning of the dreams it sends and is happy to offer clarification. But as with all dreams, expect a symbolic answer instead of a literal one.

Make It Personal

Pay attention to your speaking habits. Write down the metaphors and figures of speech you use or hear a lot, and compare them with your dreams. Are you "happy as a clam"? Or "living the dream"? You might even recognize the metaphors and figures of speech right away the next time your dreams speak to you this way, and when you do, the meaning of the dream will be more obvious.

How to Approach Nightmares

If dreams are inherently beneficial, a basic premise of this book, then why have nightmares? Why scare yourself by picturing your own death or the death of a loved one, being chased down by something sinister, or replaying the most painful and traumatizing scenes of your life? Because it is necessary for motivation, healing, or perspective.

Clever coaches know how to push the buttons of their players and get the best performance out of them, and the dream coach is a clever motivator. If you won't fight your own battles, dreams bring the fight to you. Face your fears while awake or face them when exaggerated into monsters in nightmares—the choice is yours. Nightmares have that potential to motivate, generally used as a last resort after gentler methods fail.

For healing, nightmares are an opportunity to replay and reprocess bad experiences and come out better. For example, when someone who was abused in waking life dreams of besting his or her abuser, it is a sign of moving forward. It allows parts trapped in the past to come into the present, bringing energy and zest. Trauma creates pockets of negative energy that store in the body and mind, so as a self-regulating function, dreams try to release it. Nightmares are a dramatic way of jarring it loose.

For perspective, nightmares show what is out of balance in a person. The exaggeration of a nightmare is actually an attempt at balance by graphically portraying it. Good fiction uses the same method to create a memorable story. Take for example the Flannery O'Connor short story "Everything That Rises Must Converge." It is set in the Deep South during desegregation, on a bus that only recently allowed blacks to ride, and features a white mother and her son. The mother, raised to be racist in the old South, is full of self-importance based on her perceptions of racial superiority, while her son represents the changing racial attitudes of the time. As a symbol of her self-importance, the mother wears a garish, elaborate hat. So who else gets on the bus wearing the same hat but a black mother with her son. Exact. Same. Hat. The juxtaposition makes for wicked satire as the white mother's notions are paraded before her eyes.

Think of a nightmare, then, as that hat: an exaggeration of fear, a symbol of ego inflation or willful ignorance, a painful realization about negative attitudes or beliefs. Face it while awake or face it while asleep. The psyche is supposed to balance, and if the ego drives to one extreme, the unconscious mind is sure to go just as far in the other direction.

Exaggerated Fear

Here is a nightmare that goes to one extreme because the dreamer is going another. It uses exaggeration to get its message across and recurs multiple times.

I am chased by a T. rex. I can avoid attracting its attention, but my friends don't recognize the danger and make noise. I crawl into the smallest space I can find and hope the T. rex. doesn't notice me as it sniffs around nearby.

I think the dreamer is a teenage boy, maybe ninth grade, and I begin by asking myself, what on earth is symbolized by the T. rex, an über-predator? Older authority figures are sometimes called "dinosaurs" (it doesn't matter if the dreamer uses the expression, only that he is aware of it). Thinking of the dinosaur as a symbol for an older authority figure, the rest of the dream makes sense. Old dinosaurs meddle in the lives of teenagers under their care.

The dinosaur could also be a symbol for an emotional predator—pathological personalities are like reptiles: remorseless, single-minded, and solely concerned with their own survival—but that's not what I see in the dinosaur's actions. T. rex only pokes around; it is the dreamer's reaction that is most telling. The authority figure could be a grandfather (that is what I pictured) or a teacher, coach, or father.

Nightmares like these are sometimes projections of the dreamer's fears, and you see in the dreamer's reaction to hide from T. rex that he fears something, probably scrutiny. By attracting as little attention to himself as possible, seen in the dream as crawling into the smallest space he can find, the teen figures out how to dodge the "dinosaur's" attention. But I can imagine that his friends sometimes say stuff that draws suspicion, illustrated in the dream when they make noise that attracts the dinosaur. Next thing the dreamer knows, he might be under suspicion of getting high because a friend's eyes are red, or something like that. Doesn't matter that the friend had just been swimming, the old dinosaur is suspicious of everyone—especially teenagers!

The dreamer never responded to my interpretation, so I don't know for sure what T. rex represents in his waking life, but it is most likely a fear. Other possibilities include a phobia, a painful memory, or a neglected part of himself that stalks his sleep.

Tip

Some nightmares are caused by bad diet or indigestion. Eating healthier food, and avoiding heavy, spicy foods or sweets at least two hours before bedtime will sometimes stop nightmares.

Disaster or Apocalypse

Another popular theme of nightmares is disaster or apocalypse, and it almost always represents a personal apocalypse. I asked on a discussion forum in late 2011 why more people are dreaming about apocalypse, wondering if it foretold events to come, and someone finally pointed out the obvious: More people have been experiencing "apocalypses" like losing homes and jobs since the financial meltdown in 2008—of course it shows up symbolically in dreams! The next dream is pretty typical of a personal apocalypse.

I'm in a big city and a volcano erupts nearby, devastating the city. I see lava in the streets and people trapped, dying. The scene shifts, and later I see the city flooded with seawater and people getting back on their feet.

I know of no better metaphor for explosive anger than a volcano, and an erupting volcano shows what happens when anger is no longer held down. "Blow your top" expresses this idea, and so does "have a meltdown." When bottled-up anger is suddenly let loose, it is followed by an outpouring of unconscious content, like the flood in the dream. The gates open and everything suppressed gushes forth, causing devastation in the dreamer's life, symbolized by the ruined city. But it cools the temper, a classic pattern seen in people with explosive anger. Someone doesn't actually have to "blow his top" to dream of it—he only needs to feel like it could happen. In my experience dreams are as likely to predict where you are headed as describe where you have been.

Really bad nightmares make the heart pound and the mind race. There is a feeling that your life is on the line, in danger of some terrible fate out of a horror movie. You wake startled, edgy, crying. I used to have terrifying dreams of falling and would wake up before hitting ground. One night I fell all the way and felt the first moment of hard impact. I woke up sore and feeling bruised. It was a good sign: I'd finally "hit bottom," and began to turn my life around.

The most terrifying of all nightmares can involve a parent dying. This dreamer reported it as the worst nightmare he ever had.

Mom Hanged During Apocalypse

Outside my house is the apocalypse. The planet is about to be destroyed by a meteor. Mom and I hide in the basement. I go upstairs to check on something, and when I come back she has hanged herself! It's terrible! I try to get help, but the people I find don't want to get involved. When I come back to the basement she is alive and says she never wanted to die.

So then the meteor is about to strike, but it's really an attack by aliens that want to take over. The planet turns red like Mars. Suddenly I'm in a village surrounded by the dead bodies of people who didn't survive. I'm lucky I'm not one of them. I'm hungry so I break into a store and steal some food and money, then go buy some candy. The guy selling it is greedy, and acts like all he cares about is my money.

The dreamer's biggest fear is losing his parents, so right away I see that fear symbolized in his hanged mother. There is a lot more at work here, though. The apocalypse outside his house implies a sudden, bad change in his life. The dreamer says his relationship with his mother is fine, so whatever threatens their relationship is probably hidden; it's a potential threat, something one of them knows about but the other doesn't.

The basement setting says this dream comes from the gut, where anxieties and fears can manifest. "In the basement" can also mean feelings or perceptions that are pushed out of mind. Seeing his mom hanged might make the dreamer wonder if she is suicidal—dreams can warn about loved ones contemplating suicide—but in his dream it is a symbol for something not getting through to his head. Hanging kills by cutting off circulation to the head, and symbolically it can represent anything "choked off," like feelings or thoughts. When his mother says she never wanted to die, it shows that the choice is his, not hers; she is not the source of the threat to their relationship.

The threat to their relationship, introduced first as an apocalyptic meteor strike, turns out to be aliens coming to take over the planet. Here the dream defines it. Alien is anything outside or foreign, and an alien takeover in this case means that something alien has taken over the dreamer's life. It removes the dreamer from his normal life, as seen in the sudden transition to the village, implying a more primitive condition. And it causes great internal conflict, as seen in the dead bodies piled up. It is also risky.

The Mars reference could be to aggression, since Mars is associated with war, and the Earth turned red is another reason to think the dreamer's anger or aggression is involved in the life situation described by the dream. It can also be a warning that the path he is on is likely to end in a bloody mess. You'll learn why in a moment.

The end of the dream is the real giveaway. After the dreamer has been through an apocalypse he reacts how? He says he is hungry, but this hunger isn't for food. If so, he would have been content after stealing food from the store. No, he buys "candy," and that means a vice, probably a drug habit. Adult candy costs a lot, and buying it involves people who only want your money. The greedy man at the end of the dream is a projection of this side of the dreamer. The threat symbolized by the meteor, the aliens, and the involuntary hanging of his mother stems from the dreamer's involvement in illegal drugs.

I wasn't sure about the interpretation until I read another dream from the same dreamer involving the purchase of fruit from some Mexicans in the desert. To me that means buying drugs, probably cannabis, because the fruit or bud of the plant is sold and smoked, and meeting Mexicans in the desert is a stereotypical setting for drug deals. The dreamer never responded to my interpretation.

The next nightmare is also unforgettable.

The dream is split screen. On the left screen I'm tied to a chair in the middle of a road, darkness in all directions as far as I can see. Immediately around me are burning buildings, rusted and decayed. In the streets are dismembered bodies, arms, legs, and entrails. On the right screen I'm at a formal dinner party, socializing and drinking with peers. I'm older, and I know that the future me on the right screen is responsible for everything that happens to me on the left screen.

Talk about living a double life! The symbolism of this dream is so clear. The left screen shows one half of the dreamer's life going up in flames, which was the case in the dreamer's waking life at the time of the dream. The gore and destruction are exaggerated but apt representations of a life dramatically falling apart. However, the dreamer is an ambitious social climber, and that crowd has no idea what is happening in the other half of his life. What they see is the attractive, glib man they meet at social occasions, the guy on the right side of the screen who seems to have it all together.

He is responsible for the destruction on the left because he sustains the dual existence willfully. The theme here is similar to the movie *A Clockwork Orange*, tied to a chair and forced to confront the uncomfortable truth of one's existence. By accepting the truths exposed by the dream, the dreamer can bring the two sides of his life back together as one. Because the guy on the right is shown as an older version of the dreamer, it seems to suggest that the scene is a prediction of where the dreamer is headed.

Nightmares about Current Events/the Outside World

While most nightmares are drawn from personal experience, some describe group situations. The Arab Spring of 2011, followed by the Occupy Wall Street protests in the fall, sparked dreams in response, a number of which came to my attention. It's easy to assume that dreams stick to describing your life and the people in it—but don't miss the larger implications of a dream. Dreams can also illustrate your reactions to, and feelings about, outside events, and sometimes even predict them. In the next dream I see hints of connection to events of the time, but it is the dreamer who interprets it as a graphic warning about what she fears could happen.

I am part of a team that watches out for isolated giants covered in black antimatter blotches like smoke. Once they activate, the only hope for survival is to run away, because the giants tear apart and eat people. There is tension within the team because some members don't take the threat seriously. Even though the giants move slowly, it's still awful and feels inescapable. I'm scared and don't want any part of this; I don't trust I can get away.

I initially relate this dream to encounters with dangerous people or situations but keep coming back to the giants and what they represent to the dreamer. There are forces in the world that tear apart and eat people. Some work environments can be described as meat grinders, with seemingly inhuman bosses who make life hell for everyone under their authority. I also relate the giants to the impersonal forces of Wall Street and capitalism that tear apart lives with no regard, and it rings a bell with the dreamer.

What she sees in the giants are the centers of financial and military power behind institutions like Wall Street. The dreamer fears that the bloodshed was a drop in a bucket compared to what would happen if real power moved to protect its interests. Even though she is well-informed, symbolized by being on a team of watchers, she is not always taken seriously, symbolized by dissent in the ranks of the observation team. It might even symbolize dissent within herself over the danger presented by these impersonal forces.

Nightmares generally diminish in frequency as we age, a result of how things scary to children are better understood by adults.

No monsters live in the closet. Nothing is waiting under the bed to attack when you fall asleep. Or is it? If "under the bed" symbolizes the subconscious, and going to sleep is when barriers are down, maybe something is waiting that *feels* nightmarish. Adults have their share of fears and divisions and horrors, too. As fears are faced, divisions are healed, and horrors are left behind, nightmares go away on their own. Face whatever haunts you and it no longer has power to disrupt your sleep.

Tip

Embrace your nightmares as opportunities for personal growth; don't run from them.

Recurring Dreams: Why We Have Them, How to Use Them

Dreams can tell the same story a thousand times. When we see the same story told the same way over and over, it's a recurring dream. These dreams are often reported to me with duress. Why, the dreamers ask, do they repeat? Because the dream is making a point that the dreamer isn't getting, or a condition is ongoing in daily life and has become chronic. An important, time-sensitive message is trying to get through!

While a series of dreams can come along every few months and last for several nights in a row, recurring dreams don't move forward; you remain stuck in the same scenario until you make the correct decision, or until the dreaming mind moves on to other tactics to get your attention, like nightmares. In general, the more urgent the dream, the more urgent its message—and the more you are likely to repeat it until its message is received.

Some of the dreams we have looked at already are of the recurring variety, like the T. rex dream (see page 91). It recurs because the dreamer's situation, being watched over by a "dinosaur," doesn't change, and neither do his feelings about it.

Here is another example of a recurring dream.

Every night lately I've had the same dream: My wedding ring is too big and slips off my finger. I wake up no matter what time it is, worried.

A wedding ring can be a symbol for marriage or any big commitment and all it entails. In this case, a wedding ring that is too big and slips off the finger is a metaphor for the role or responsibilities of marriage feeling too big for the dreamer. That is a hard fact to admit, but if ignored it is likely to lead to separation.

The resolution in this dream is implied by the problem presented and the obvious need to do something about it; first, though, some feelings have to be acknowledged. The dreamer has been ignoring the warnings that his marriage feels too big for him, so the dreams recur. After working through those feelings and deciding he will do whatever it takes to save his marriage, he dreams this:

I dream again that my wedding ring is too big, and decide to put it in an ornate box under my pillow for safekeeping while I go to the gym, thinking that building muscle will fatten my finger.

The recurring dreams move forward once the dreamer gets the message. What happens next is a good sign for his marriage: He stores the ring for safekeeping until he "fits" the marriage it symbolizes. Storing the ring under his pillow means he still "dreams" of a successful marriage, since a pillow is an object the head rests on while dreaming.

The gym is a setting for self-improvement, and while he might go to the gym more in waking life to improve his physical condition and relieve stress, as a dream symbol it can mean other sorts of improvements, such as regularly doing chores, or setting up a system so that he never forgets a birthday or anniversary.

Character and mind can be exercised and improved the same as body. The dreamer's reaction shows he is willing to make the effort to save his marriage.

Now consider if the dreamer had reacted to the problem of his wedding ring being too big by resizing it. What does it say about him? Probably that he would rather change the relationship than grow into it.

Here is another recurring dream:

My apartment is filled with people just hanging out, partying and talking. The small living room is packed with strangers. I don't want them there, but I'm afraid of causing a scene by telling them to leave. Why do I have this dream night after night?

The dreamer, a male in his late twenties, is active socially and frequently has people over to hang out at his apartment. He enjoys being a center of social activity, but deep down he knows that maintaining his wide circle of friends and acquaintances takes away from private time, expressed in the dream by the feeling that he wants the crowd to leave. The crowded living room further illustrates the dreamer's dilemma because it is the space where he "lives," the place in his mind where he spends most of his time and a symbol for his living situation, and it's overrun by the many people in his life. In the dream he is afraid of causing a scene, interpreted as fear that restricting his social life means solitude.

Here is how the dream progresses once the conflict of the recurring dream is acknowledged and resolved:

I come back to my apartment and police officers haul away the party crowd. The police are sort of friendly as they go about their business. I notice the tattoos and shaggy hair of the people leaving my apartment.

The original dreams ask the dreamer to create a less crowded situation for himself, not become a hermit. He can always seek out excitement and friends at a pub or other social scene, but he needs his home environment to himself. The negativity associated with his life being too crowded, symbolized by the shaggy hair and tattoos of the people hauled away, is cleared out when he closes off his living space.

Once he makes the decision to honor his need for space, a powerful part of the psyche symbolized by the police in the dream is enabled to do the grunt work of cleaning up after the party. Edgar Cayce, a psychic and dream interpreter who became famous during the first half of the twentieth century for prescribing miraculous medical cures, calls it the "superconscious." Sigmund Freud calls it the "superego," and both words describe the part of the person strongly focused on right and wrong. Some people live their lives closely tied to it, like religious fundamentalists, and others hide from or deny it. The superconscious is meant to balance with the rest of the mind. It can just as readily place too many restrictions on a person as help restrain impulses and bad habits.

The police are an example of independent actors in the mind that come to the dreamer's aid when given the ability. The saying "heaven helps those who help themselves" speaks to this relationship between action and aid. Help yourself by doing the right thing and the superconscious is enabled to clear the personal space needed for good decision making. When you are ready to act on what your dreams advise, they offer help from the inside.

This self-help from within is another reason why understanding dreams is so important. Otherwise, the dreamer in the last example doesn't restrict his living space. His conflicted feelings become chronic because the original dream isn't resolved, and the police never come to clean out his internal space if he doesn't first invite them.

Make It Personal

If you have recurring dreams, look for situations that are ongoing, espe-cially ones that cause anxiety, stress, or fear. The only good way to resolve recurring dreams is to address the underlying situation, and if it can't be changed, find a way to be at peace with it. Pleasant dreams can recur also, but the dreams that cause distress are the ones I run across most frequently in dream forums and conversations. They are dreams that require immediate attention and don't have to be interpreted before acted on.

If you are bothered by recurring nightmares or unpleasant dreams and can't figure out what they speak to, work backward by examining your life. You know something is out of whack and needs to be addressed, and you know that nightmares are exag-gerations of feelings, fears, anxieties, and bad situations. Just by working with the dreams, you enable the unconscious side of the mind to give aid from behind the scenes, so even if working backward doesn't lead to a correct interpretation, it might solve the underlying issue simply by giving yourself extra attention.

How to Know an Interpretation Is on Target

Only you know what your dreams mean, so only you know when an interpretation rings true. With all the possibilities presented by every dream, pinning down an interpretation can be mad-deningly difficult. Dreams layer meaning, speaking to different areas of life, and for rationalists who must have concrete ground to work on, dream interpretation runs counter to the way their minds work. That's not to say that dreams can't be verified—but it won't satisfy the requirements of hard science. As long as you, the author of the dream, think an interpretation is correct, that is all that matters.

I use three primary ways to verify an interpretation is on target:

- It feels right.

- It's consistent with other dreams.

- It's proven correct by subsequent experience.

When someone has been working hard to figure out a dream and it suddenly makes sense, the reaction is almost audible. Subconsciously, you already know everything that happens in a dream beforehand, because you are the author of the story and the material is drawn from your life. Your mind makes this stuff up—doesn't it make sense that you know what your dreams mean, subconsciously or not? A dream interpreter's job, then, is to tell you what you already know, running through possibilities until something "clicks," and that happens when the interpretation feels right.

The second way of verifying is basic science. If you have data to compare the dream to, do it. In this sense your dream journal is also your database. After a while you will notice patterns that are unlikely to be recognized from memory alone; a catalog of dream material is needed. Sometimes a dream interpretation can be verified by comparing it to other dreams from the same night. It may be that all dreams are connected to tell one story even if they seem unrelated. For an in-depth look at a dream of this type, see "Mafia Slave" (page 208).

A pattern in my dreams involves a married couple I've known since college. They appear in dreams about recreational drinking because that is what we enjoyed doing together, the activity central to our relationship. Even though I haven't seen them in years, they still appear in my dreams when the subject involves our favorite pastime.

Similarly, you can rule out interpretations that are not consistent with other dreams. If I dream about going to Paris (see page 10), I know I'm not dreaming about the need for a vacation, but rather about the need for intellectual or romantic pursuits.

A correct interpretation will sometimes be verified by subsequent experience. If, for example a dream warns against a romantic relationship with a particular person but the dreamer moves forward with it anyway, I'll bet the dream is right and the dreamer will regret ignoring the warning. I cannot think of one example of someone who took the advice of a dream and it turned out to be wrong. You know a dream interpretation is correct when it serves its purpose: benefiting your life.

Dreams have been known to foretell future events, either by projecting where current patterns are leading or by actually seeing the future. Most of the time it is coincidence, but in some instances it appears that dreams are accurate to the last detail in ways that can't be coincidence. This is the ultimate way of verifying a dream. We'll go into more detail on this subject in the next step.

Make It Personal

Let's interpret one of your dreams using the process I have shown you. Choose a dream from your journal, one you remember in detail, and break it down into its elements:

- Symbolism:

- Setting(s):

- Character(s):

Now break down the story to its components:

- Action:

- Reaction:

- Resolution:

1. Look at each element. Ask what it describes and what it can be compared to. Ask if it is more likely to describe your internal or external life. If the characters and settings remind you of a recent event or situation, the dream is more likely to be about your external life, and you should first focus your attention there. If they don't appear to have any connection, the dream is more likely to be about your internal life. Dreams that mix the unfamiliar with the familiar might show the connections between your internal and external life. Think about your recent life, especially the day before having the dream, and look for connections with the dream in the events and situations you experienced, and in your thoughts and feelings.

2. Next, look at the components. The action tells the story and is often symbolic, especially when you do something out of character. Your reaction tells you how you would respond under the circumstances or how you wish you could respond. The resolution is where you are most likely to find answers and suggestions. It might be symbolic, or it might be up to you to dream up your own resolution.

3. Make associations. For external dreams you associate mainly with the people and situations in your life. For internal dreams you associate mainly with yourself and your feelings. But remember that there isn't always a clear divide, so let your associations roam free. They are your main tool for interpreting your dreams.

4. Associate with the symbolism. Look up the symbols in part II of this book, "A User's Guide to Dream Symbolism," and/or in other sources. Ask yourself how the symbolism helps tell the story. Does it connect the elements and components? Remember that pretty much everything in your dreams is symbolic, and the way dreams express meaning is usually through the action. Work with the symbols, settings, and characters by asking what they remind you of, where you have seen them, and what they mean to you.

5. Look for metaphors. Look for story threads. Look for wordplay.

6. If the meaning of the dream is not revealed this way, go further by speaking from the perspective of the puzzling parts.

7. And finally, be patient! Dreams aren't always decipherable right away, but persistence pays off.

Your effort to remember and interpret your dreams will be rewarded with a new understanding of yourself and your world, which is certainly something to be excited about. I emphasize effort because learning to remember, interpret, and live your dreams takes time and energy. If you see the point of it, the effort comes naturally. You are Alice chasing the Rabbit to discover your own Wonderland. If you don't see the point, you won't expend the energy. Any effort to work with your dreams is worth it in the long run; it's a marathon, not a sprint.

Now that you know enough to remember and interpret your dreams, you are ready for the third step. Living your dreams is, after all, the point of remembering and interpreting them.

Live Your Dreams

"Live your dreams" is more than a cliché; it is the best advice for living a full life. As you can see by now, dreams present all sorts of beneficial information about you and your life. So what does "live your dreams" really mean? It boils down to four key points:

1. Remember and interpret your dreams.

2. Recognize their importance.

3. Take their advice and suggestions.

4. Work with them consciously during the day.

The more you work with your dreams, the stronger the connection grows between the unconscious and conscious sides of the mind, and the easier it becomes to remember and interpret them. You live your dreams by incorporating them into your daily life, not by limiting them to your sleeping hours.

Dreams are the ultimate life coach, an adviser that sees you inside and out, is there for all the ups and downs, and knows what you really want and how to make it happen. Dream about where you want to go and who you want to be, and follow the trail while awake.

Dreams are life coaches in a broader sense, too, through the wisdom imparted. It is saturnine wisdom that breaks down illusions and exposes what is hidden. No excuses are needed, only a dispassionate look at your life and a desire to better it. Your perceptions deepen. Patterns are easier to identify. People are easier to read. Solutions come more readily to mind. Situations are more readily handled.

Beyond personal development, the dream coach helps answer the question of what you really want. That question is difficult when the answer is "everything" or "no idea." Dreams identify the road that leads to the most fulfillment, health, and happiness, as seen from the broader perspective of the unconscious mind. They can even see ahead and prepare for the future, and aid in your endeavors and creations. Consider some of the great creations and discoveries credited to dreams:

- The periodic table was first seen in dream by Dmitri Mendeleev.
- Paul McCartney credits the Beatles song "Yesterday" to a dream.
- The first patented sewing machine in America was invented by Elias Howe after dreaming spears with eyelets near the tips were being thrust at him.
- Mary Shelley's *Frankenstein* first came to life in her dreams.
- Robert Louis Stevenson had been racking his brain for a chilling plot and got it when he "dreamed up" *Strange Case of Dr. Jekyll and Mr. Hyde,* one of the most famous horror stories of all time.
- Stephen King regularly "scavenges" (as he puts it) dream material for his books, and credits the premise of his novel *Misery* to a dream.

- A dream showed Jack Nicklaus how to correct a hitch in his golf swing, clearing the way for him to tear up the course and make golf history.

- Einstein's theory of relativity came to him in a dream.

- Dr. Frederick Banting discovered insulin after dreaming about new diabetes experiments.

- The chemist August Kekule dreamed of a snake biting its tail, which supposedly revealed the chemical structure of benzene.

- The music to the Christmas carol "O Little Town of Bethlehem" was written after Lewis Henry Redner woke up in the middle of the night and heard what he said was an "angel-strain" whispering in his ear. Was it an angel, a dream, or an angel in a dream?

- Salvador Dalí's surrealist paintings are basically all from dreams.

- Films like Christopher Nolan's *Inception,* David Lynch's *Blue Velvet,* and Stanley Kubrick's *Eyes Wide Shut* (based on Arthur Schnitzler's 1926 novella *Dream Story*) were all inspired by dreams.

- Tabitha Babbitt invented the circular saw when she dreamed of a sewing machine and saw combined.

- Hannibal, one of the most famous generals in history, used strategies from his dreams to defeat the Romans.

These dreams made history. Most are mundane in comparison. However, one really important dream can set the course of a lifetime, like Albert Einstein's dream of a roller coaster that opened his understanding of relativity. (Einstein regularly used his dreams to solve physics problems.) Just as important are the dreams that work through issues of the day and lead to a better understanding of oneself, because a lot of little dreams precede the life-changing ones, and what may seem like small steps in understanding them can lead to big leaps and sudden breakthroughs.

We hear about the famous examples of books, inventions, scientific breakthroughs, or works of art inspired by dreams, but every day people solve problems, answer questions, address issues, and open up new opportunities with the help of their dreams.

I saw a terrific example of this in December 2010, when I was watching the annual Oregon vs. Oregon State football game on TV. The broadcast crew found a popular local eatery packed with fans rooting for their teams and scarfing down pub food. The reporter related a story from the owner of the eatery about the inspiration for opening the business coming from a dream. The owner woke up at 3:00 in the morning with the concept, name, and logo in mind, and soon after embarked on a career as a restaurateur. It turned out to be a great decision for himself, his family, and the community.

Sometimes dreams are very literal, as was the case with the owner of the Oregon eatery. Sometimes they are not so clear. Every day, someone somewhere wakes up with an inspiration that changes his or her life or even the world in some way. I know an inventor who holds dozens of patents for dream-inspired creations. Musicians write entire songs in their sleep; painters see their next paintings; advertisers dream up campaigns; computer programmers devise new software; carpenters design their next creations. Dreams can tell you which home to buy, which career to pursue, which person to befriend, which mate to marry. If Abe Lincoln had heeded the warning he received in a dream, he might have avoided assassination!

Take another example: A business manager dreams that he walks into the office and finds his employees playing musical chairs. Instead of getting angry that they aren't working, he leads the game and enjoys it. The next day he is inspired to shake things up by shifting his staff's job positions—musical chairs.

An information technology specialist who teaches yoga at night dreams that he turns his backyard into an outdoor yoga area to accommodate a group of students. The idea strikes him as something he would like to do. He realizes he has been keeping his yoga practice separate because his day job is so different from his night job. In this sense, yoga occupies the "backyard" of his life, and the dream tells him to put more focus and effort into it. The next morning, he brings a book about yoga to his day job and leaves it out on his desk where his coworkers can see it, a way of bringing his yoga practice out of the backyard.

Some dreams try to solve work-related issues, what you might call general problem solving. The dreaming mind is always observing and taking notes, and can make connections the conscious mind misses. This is a great example.

Following Directions on a Map

My old friend Gary from graduate school is in the passenger seat of my car giving me directions from a map he's holding. I'm not sure where we are going, but I sense it is important.

Ten years removed from graduate school, the dreamer my partner, Lisa—wondered why a former schoolmate would show up in her dream. She hadn't been particularly close with him, but they were friendly colleagues. To begin understanding why he is in the dream, we look at her present life for a place she is trying to get to that requires a "map," remembering that driving is often symbolic for "going somewhere" in life.

Lisa had been researching an idea for a book but was having trouble wrapping her mind around it. She had many ideas, many directions to go in, and felt overwhelmed. Gary had taught her during grad school how to organize big writing projects by listing topics and subtopics on index cards and then arranging them in the order she wanted. He holds a map while Lisa drives, symbolizing how his advice "maps out" where she is going. She needs a reminder that she already possesses the ability to organize her book, and her vigilant dream coach provides it.

Tip

Little good comes from knowing the meaning of a dream unless you use it to improve yourself, help someone else, or make needed changes.

The Dream Oracle

Dreams have an ESP quality, picking up information seemingly out of the air like an antenna receiving signals. This information could be the aggressive vibe of a business rival or schoolmate, or the amorous vibe of a potential lover that you're oblivious to during the day. It could be someone's actual thoughts or feelings, regardless of how long it's been since you've been in touch; the moment the phone rings you know who it is because you dreamed about the call the night before.

Here is another example of the dream oracle at work: A college-age dreamer asks his mom for money to take a road trip with his friends and she turns him down. Then that night he dreams:

My mom comes into my room and gives me sixty dollars. She says forty dollars is for food and twenty dollars is for gas.

The dreamer said that the next morning his mom changed her mind, came into his room, and gave him sixty dollars, telling him forty dollars was for food and twenty dollars was for gas—just like in the dream. I imagine she also told him to be safe and return in one piece or she'd forever feel guilty for funding the trip. It could be a coincidence, but examples of ESP dreams are countless, and that is no coincidence.

With the physical senses shut down and the conscious mind out of the way while asleep, more signals get through, beginning with whatever is missed or unresolved during the day. Therefore, working with your dreams can produce all sorts of benefits, solve problems, even help you to avoid disasters. Here is a prime example of a disaster avoided through a preemptive dream.

Finding a White Pill

I'm in my living room and notice a small white pill on the carpet under the couch. I realize it could be dangerous for my baby and pick it up.

The next morning the dreamer looked under her couch and found a white pill that might have killed her child if swallowed, located exactly where the dream told her it would be. In the same discussion, someone mentioned a dream about a spectacular Dale Earnhardt crash at a NASCAR race, and it happened months later while the dreamer was actually at the race, again exactly as he dreamed it. Another person dreamed of a scorpion hidden inside some old boxes, and he found it the next day in the exact place he dreamed it would be.

Presumably, the dream was a warning, and the dreamer's alertness saved him from getting stung. The pill under the couch dream can be explained as the mother saw the pill earlier that day out of the corner of her eye, but was too distracted to notice consciously. The Earnhardt dream can't be used as proof that some dreams foretell the future, but it is anecdotal. The scorpion is harder to explain conventionally. If you live in the desert, it's always wise to watch out for scorpions when going through stored boxes, but you could check a thousand times and never encounter one. It appears likely that the dream source somehow knew that an encounter with a scorpion was imminent.

Dreams can be prophetic, foretelling situations and events in the dreamer's life—or what *can* happen, since the dream source is very good at identifying patterns and seeing where they are leading. In that sense, dreams are less prophetic and more wise. However, some events transpire exactly as seen in a dream—or don't transpire because the person was forewarned.

In a foretelling dream that warned of danger ahead, a guy saw a blue sports car merge onto the highway and cause a horrific accident. The next morning he was driving on the highway when a blue sports car sped recklessly into traffic while merging onto the highway, almost causing an accident. The dreamer slowed down when he saw the car, instead of aggressively speeding up like he would usually be tempted to do, slowing down the drivers behind him. Accident avoided.

Another dream warned a guy about driving off the side of a mountain in an SUV he didn't recognize, with a passenger, a girl he knew. A week later he was asked to drive on a beer run after drinking at a campsite in the mountains. The car: the SUV from his dream. The passenger: the girl from his dream, the owner of the SUV. He was reminded of the dream and chose not to drive, which angered the girl and the thirsty campers, but probably saved her life and his.

We will never know for sure because the accident he dreamed about was prevented, but you can find out for yourself that dreams foretell future events—getting glimpses of the future is a widely known phenomenon in dream study circles. Keep a journal, track your dreams, and I bet you will experience it too.

In some tribal-based societies today, people believe that the future is created by dreams. Therefore, dreams are shared with the entire community and acted on like their lives and livelihoods depend on it. So in a way, the belief that dreams create the future is a self-fulfilling prophecy. If I dream of something tonight and act on it tomorrow, I have created the future through my dreams.

Some educated, scientifically minded readers will no doubt feel that dreaming the future into existence involves nothing more than coincidence or unconscious wish fulfillment, the silly belief of primitive people who lend too much importance to brain activity while asleep. It is true that dreams help sort information and store memories, and some dreams aren't worth remembering because there is nothing to interpret—they are byproducts of bodily and subconscious regulating activities, or the result of illness or bad digestion. But just because some dreams don't have meaning doesn't mean they are all meaningless (a line of reasoning often used to try to discredit dream interpretation). This would exclude the clear connections made by psychiatrists and laymen between dreams and their dreamers, dreams layered with meaning that help people understand their lives better.

The bias against meaning in dreams boils down to hardheaded denial; some people deny any meaning in dreams because they don't see the meaning or significance in their own. Or they balk at the mystical or ESP aspects. They think everything happens by chance. Creating your future in your dreams is impossible, they say.

To them I say that quantum physics has shown us how our reality is created through intelligent observation, and how energy particles exist in a sea of infinite possibility, taking form only when observed. In dreams we are shown possibilities. We make choices from among the possibilities. We observe the future taking shape and decide what it will be. I can't prove it scientifically, but I have experienced it for myself many times.

The best knowledge is personal knowledge, so find out for yourself from your dreams.

Déjà rêvé, which means "already dreamed," is when a dream is remembered because the similarity to waking life triggers the memory of it. A place never visited suddenly seems familiar because you have been there before in a dream. Or it could be a familiar setting with a certain combination of people or a particular action that triggers the memory. Either way, you know that you are living in a moment that you dreamed about first. I have even dreamed of what people were going to say in future conversations and how I should respond. It is a common experience, but most people don't remember their dreams well enough to know they've dreamed about the future. Déjà vu is a similar phenomenon tied to the dreaming mind's ability to predict the future or foresee possibilities.

In a powerful case of déjà rêvé, a guy dreamed about seeing his mother, who had passed away two years earlier, on a balcony of an unfamiliar apartment that he was cleaning. Seeing her in the dream made him burst into tears after waking up. Months later he flew to Paris for his brother's wedding. He was in his brother's apartment for the first time when he realized it was identical to the apartment from his dream. He went to the balcony and realized it was where his mother had stood.

Seeing his mom in the dream was setting him up for an important moment months down the road. His action of cleaning the apartment is symbolic of cleaning up the divisions between him and his family following her death. For her sake he should make peace.

Pay close attention during moments of déjà rêvé or déjà vu. Even if it appears ordinary, the time is ripe with possibility. Go with the flow and be extra aware of what you are feeling and the decisions you are making.

Make It Personal

Can you think of a time when your dreams have shown you possibilities for your future? Or when you have experienced déjà vu or déjà rêvé? Write down the details in your journal. Tracking this information can lead to better recognition of what your dreams tell you and enhance your ability to use this information constructively. It also tells your unconscious mind that you will put in the effort, leading to more opportunities to shape your future through your dreams.

Using Dreams for Personal Growth

Somewhere in every meaningful dream is the potential for personal growth. Simply giving it attention aids a subconscious process of integrating experiences and setting up scenarios for your personal development. As we've discussed, your dreams give you clues about their meaning through the settings, characters, symbols, actions, reactions, and especially resolutions. The resolution of a dream is often where suggestions are made, advice is given, or new perspectives are revealed. Look at the resolution of a dream first for ways to bring your dreams into your daily life.

Every day, I want you to try to live your dreams in meaningful ways. You might try thinking about a dream and replaying it in your mind. Review recent dreams before going to bed. By thinking about dreams as part of your regular routine, you open more links between the conscious and unconscious sides of your mind, and the information that used to be communicated in dramatic, sometimes nightmarish dreams will flow more readily. You'll find you don't need a nightmare to get the message across.

You will also become better at recognizing moments in daily life that are first seen in your dreams. When you're tuned in and paying close attention, seeing your future can be an everyday occurrence. Ironically, dreams often show you future moments that don't appear on the surface to be significant. From the perspective of your dreams, the external events of your life are less important than the internal ones.

Your dreams give you images or motifs to work with that can be made part of yourself or your living environment. An especially vivid and powerful dream I had long ago involved getting a tattoo of a wolf on my left shoulder. When I woke up the next morning, my shoulder felt sore, like I'd actually gotten a tattoo.

That dream opened my eyes to seeing the wolf as a living part of me. I studied wolves and found ways I relate to them, and even years later I still remember the dream like it just happened. I worked to strengthen the connection between myself and the wolf, and my life was enriched by personally identifying with it.

One woman dreamed of a frog turned inside out, its guts spilled. Knowing that frogs can be a symbol for a person's inner nature, I thought it was wise for the dreamer to identify with the frog and recommended she buy a figurine or something to remind her of it. By consciously directing energy at the frog image, the dreamer was actually caring for and protecting her shy, sensitive side. You could pay thousands of dollars to a psychiatrist to accomplish the same goal using other techniques, but your dreams provide everything you need to do it yourself.

Another person wanted to know why he dreamed about a girl from college. In the dream they hung out, talked, and had a great time together. He felt there was chemistry between them in the dream. Nothing sexual happened. The dreamer told me he had noticed the girl previously and thought she was attractive, but soon school was over for the summer and he went home. The next fall, just as school started, he had the dream. At the risk of giving bad advice, I suggested he look her up. The dream seemed to suggest they might make good friends at the very least. He said she reminded him of his only serious relationship, which he broke off because his girlfriend turned clingy. I suggested the girl in his dream might remind him of why he was attracted to his ex-girlfriend, and the easy interaction in the dream seemed to indicate that the new girl was not the clingy type.

A word to the wise: Don't take the fact that someone was in your dream as a sign of attraction or natural chemistry. People you know in waking life can appear in your dreams for all sorts of reasons. To reach the conclusion with the dream just described, I took into account the action and the dreamer's association with his ex-girlfriend. I had a feeling he might be scanning his environment for a girlfriend, and his dream made a suggestion based on what it knew. However, because there was nothing sexual or romantic in the dream, it might have suggested the girl as a step in the right direction: Maybe by being just friends with this girl and eschewing the romance, at least initially, he could learn a needed relationship skill. Either way, I thought he should go for it.

Tip

If you have something on your mind, ask your dreams to send you an answer. Some people like to write their question or request on a piece of paper and sleep with it under their pillow. Only ask one question at a time.

There are several other creative ways you can work with dreams in your daily life. Overviews of some of them are given next. I encourage you to find personal ways to honor and work with your dreams, remembering there are no right or wrong ways, only your way, and the more effort you put in, the more you gain.

Active Imagination

Dreams and imagination share the same brain space. In fact, a dream is essentially your imagination at work while the conscious side of your brain rests. Therefore, you can use your imagination to actively reenter, add to, or alter your dreams, and your mind won't know the difference. (Note: "Active imagination" is basically the same as "creative visualization." It's the same process with different terminology depending on if it's used with a dream or with something from your waking life.)

For instance, if you don't like the way a dream ends, imagine it turning out better. I had one such dream of an angry man in my attic, mentioned previously (page 18). I woke up feeling upset and disappointed with myself, questioning what made me respond to him angrily. I reentered the dream later that day, vividly picturing the scenes while relaxed in a quiet place, eyes closed, breathing deeply and slowly through my nose. In my mind I saw the angry man and apologized for reacting instead of listening. I asked him to tell me why he was angry, and he responded by telling me I wasn't paying attention to his needs.

That statement led me to connect the man with my inner child, and I realized I was neglecting regular meals and sleep. I had been working really hard for several days straight and justified not taking care of myself because I had my nose to the grindstone. In my mind I could see the child side of myself and his needs inside the angry man. That night I went to bed at my regular time rather than work late, and the next morning, rather than jumping on my computer first thing and getting back to work, I was sure to eat a good breakfast first. My reaction satisfied the angry man, because he didn't appear again in my dreams after that.

Tip

When dream characters transform before your eyes, they are showing you what they really are, what they symbolize. For example, a big monster that turns into a mouse when confronted might symbolize how small causes are often behind big fears.

The way I describe the process makes it appear to be neat and linear, but it isn't. It took a while to get the man to speak to me, and the connection with my inner child popped into my head after analyzing my initial reaction. Because I kept the dream in mind and worked with it, I got the ball rolling. I didn't understand the meaning right away, and didn't need to: I figured out the message of the dream by paying attention, making connections with waking life—especially with my feelings—and working with it in my imagination.

Active imagination often involves engaging in conversation with dream characters, questioning them about their roles and pumping them for information. It only works if you are willing to wait patiently for a response and listen when it comes. When working with your dreams, leave behind your impatience, frustration, guilt, and excuses, and be open to what your subconscious is trying to tell you.

You can also use your imagination to alter disturbing scenes, such as the one in this dream:

I am with my older brother and there is this young kid who wants to join us as we walk around town looking for something. The kid must be foreign or something because he talks with an accent. My brother tells him to come along with us. We find a gun that looks like my brother's, and when I touch it, it turns into a butterfly knife. I try disassembling it and get cut by a sharp piece inside of it.

Then all of a sudden we are in my bedroom and I am just waking up. The boy is in my bed and cut all through the stomach, blood and guts everywhere. My brother is there and hands me a knife to finish the job of killing him. I think to myself, "This must be a dream, and if it's a dream I can do anything. I can heal the boy—heal everyone!" Then I wake up for real.

There's some powerful mojo at work in this dream. It opens by showing the older brother's influence on the dreamer. What they are looking for as they walk around town is where the young kid—a projection of a side of the dreamer, the kid side that is still innocent and easily influenced—fits into the picture. The reference to the kid being foreign is a sign that the dreamer feels that this side of himself does not belong in his relationship with his brother, probably because little kids aren't usually welcome around tough guys who run around looking for guns.

The gun might symbolize a self-image based on the idea that people who carry guns are tough and cool. Then the gun changes to a butterfly knife, a fancy weapon used on the streets by people who take their knives seriously. Transformation from one thing into another in a dream is a way of showing what it really symbolizes.

Because the gun looks like one his brother carries, I interpret the dream as a story about a younger brother emulating his older brother. The older brother is a tough guy. The younger brother wants to be a tough guy too, so by looking for a gun, in a sense he is looking to be like his brother. However, he cuts himself when he disassembles the gun, meaning he is trying to be someone he is not. The gun and what it represents aren't meant for him. This interpretation also connects him with the young boy in the next scene who bleeds all over the bed.

The dreamer's innocent side is being murdered, symbolized by the boy cut to shreds in the bed, and the dreamer is expected to finish the job. This part implies that the dreamer has absorbed something from his brother's influence that is killing him inside. However, there is hope because the young boy is still alive at the end of the dream.

The most important part is at the end when the dreamer realizes he can heal the boy, because it is a dream and he can do anything in a dream. Here is the resolution. I suggested that the dreamer use active imagination to reenter the dream and see himself heal the boy. If he could imagine it in a way that made it feel real, my hope was he could also bring healing into his life and save the part of himself that was vanishing under the influence of his brother. Kill off your inner child and you kill off the side of yourself that approaches life with wonder and enthusiasm.

Tip

According to psychologist Robert A. Johnson, the unconscious mind has two means of communicating with its conscious counterpart: dreams and imagination. Therefore, you can use your imagination to gain the same benefits as dreaming.

Here is another dream that provides helpful images for use with active imagination:

I am on a beach where a campfire is lit. There is a girl facing a wall with her back turned, and a group of mean girls behind her throw gummy worms that stick to the wall.

The beach is the meeting place of land and sea and can therefore symbolize where the conscious and unconscious sides of the mind meet, in this case to pass along information. A fire is a sort of illumination that shows what is happening inside the dreamer, in her feelings. It can also symbolize feelings that "burn." The girl facing the wall is a projection of a side of the dreamer that feels ashamed of who she is, which is why she faces the wall. The mean girls behind her are the nagging voices in her head that tell her she is somehow less female than they are.

The resulting thoughts that attack her self-image are symbolized by gummy worms. Because negative thoughts have a way of burrowing into the mind, they are compared to worms. The sticky part shows how negative thoughts and perceptions are sticky; once they take hold in the mind, they are hard to get rid of and difficult to "chew" or process. The fact that the mean girls throw gummy worms shows that the girls symbolize the source of negativity.

To use active imagination with this dream, I suggested the dreamer intervene by imagining a barrier between the mean girls and their target, and inserting herself into the picture to tell the shunned girl she has nothing to be ashamed of; to the contrary, she has more going for her than the mean girls do, and she can rid her life of what they represent by asserting herself against the feelings of shame and affirming her self-worth.

By using her imagination to work with the dream and make it turn out better, the dreamer activates an unconscious process with waking life benefits. The ball starts rolling toward healing the negative self-image portrayed by the dream. The dream takes something negative in her life and turns it into a story for her to work with and learn from, to heal and move on. She resolves the dream by using her imagination to visualize a solution, and persuading a dream character to participate in the healing process.

Active imagination was popularized by Carl Jung and his students, and is a commonly recommended technique not only for working with dreams, but any area of life. It is used today as creative visualization in athletics to visualize game-winning performance, or in sales strategy to visualize a sale being made, two of many examples. Jung's student Robert A. Johnson wrote a popular book titled *Inner Work: Using Dreams and Active Imagination for Personal Growth*. I highly recommend it if you'd like to know more about the subject.

The dream work techniques described next are extensions of active imagination.

Make It Personal

Can you think of a dream you'd like to change for the better? Then do so right now. First, make sure you are relaxed and free of distraction. Then fully immerse yourself in the scene, using your imagination to make the story work out better for all involved, even the "bad guys." Tap into the inner power you have to create harmony inside yourself and outside yourself. Just don't force anything; the scary and disturbing parts of your dreams are loaded with potential to effect changes in your life, but the challenges they present must be met head-on.

Inner Dialogue

Inner dialogue is as simple as holding a conversation with yourself, a question and answer session. Most people think of themselves as "I," but from the viewpoint of the unconscious mind, you are "we," a collection of parts overseen and held together by an ego (or not). Those parts will personify as dream characters or other symbols, and you can ask the characters (or any symbol) why they are in your dream and what you can learn from them. Have these conversations after waking up, or even while still dreaming.

Don't expect the characters to answer you straight; they are actors playing roles, and you dialogue with them within a context. If a character presents itself to you as an honest judge, address him or her as Your Honor and act like an attorney. If the character is a physician, assume you are in front of a doctor who is there to help you with your health. If the character is a teacher, pretend you are a student or colleague. The worst thing you can do is try to force them to conform to the logic of the waking world, like this:

"Alright, Mr. Judge, or whoever you are supposed to be, I don't have much time here, so let's cut to the chase. I know you represent some side of me, and I need to know what it is. Why don't you save us all some trouble and just tell me? Hurry up, I'm listening."

The Judge isn't likely to answer, and if you do get an answer, it's likely to be "piss off." Shortcuts get you nowhere.

You can conceive this relationship however your imagination dreams up as long as it includes respect for all your dream characters. Try positioning yourself as the CEO who is first among equals, with your dream characters as the department heads. Ask questions, listen, accept advice, and give direction. You are there to gain information you don't already know. You could also try being a king or queen holding court, a NASCAR pit chief directing crew members, or the president of your own little country. Just remember that the parts of you represented by your dream characters have their own points of view and opinions, even their own feelings and thoughts, and just because they are part of you doesn't mean they can be ordered around or coerced. Gain their respect and they will gladly assist in your daily life and in your dreams, unlocking potential for personal development you might not know you have.

In a powerful dream years ago, I first learned how to dialogue with my dream characters while dreaming.

There is a knock at my front door, and without opening it, I ask who is there.

"Enemies," I hear in reply.

I open the door. Two men enter my apartment. The one in front is bigger than me and intimidating, with brown hair, a beard, and a mustache. The other one slips behind me so I don't get a full view of him. I grab a martial arts weapon and attack the first man with it. I see the weapon impact his body, but no harm is done no matter how hard I swing; he is still in my apartment and not going away until I deal with him. He says, "Anger won't help you."

At this point I become conscious I am dreaming, and the dream gets unstable. The realization startles me out of sleep. I only have time for one question, so as the dream setting fades away, I ask:

"What are your names?"

Two voices answer together, "James and John."

I asked for their names because it not only gave me an easy reference, it also provided information to use for association. James wasn't hard to identify; that is my father's name, though he goes by Jim. My father is a gentle man, but when he gets mad or feels threatened, he can fly off the handle like I did in the dream. James had facial hair like my dad, though he appeared younger in the dream because he was a side of myself that had been shaped by my father. By associating that name with the dream character and my dad's influence, I have a shorthand way of referring to a part of myself.

For several years after the dream I talked with "James" and referred to him as a living part of me, someone who came to my apartment as an enemy but was actually there to help me understand myself better. In this way I lived out the dream by making it part of my waking life.

The John character was harder to figure out. For one, I couldn't "see" him; I only got a flash of a shadowy face that seemed shifty and indulgent. Also, the only people I knew named John played no role in my life. I had to figure him out by studying his behavior.

No matter how fast I turned around in the dream, John was always directly behind me, which means he was in a blind spot; I was not aware of him and his influence in my life. Also, he attacked me where I was vulnerable, from behind, though I wasn't as concerned with him as a physical threat in the dream as I was with the bigger guy, James. I suspected John might influence me through my feelings or perceptions. I also remembered the scripture, "Get thee behind me, Satan." It's a way of saying "get out of my sight, creep."

The picture of John my dream character filled out, and one day his name finally made sense: A "John" is slang for the client of a prostitute, and at the time I was working on being more aware of sexuality's influence on me. John symbolized the side of myself that turned to sex to fill holes in my life. He used sexuality to sway my thoughts and feelings and take me in directions other than where I needed to go, hiding all the while in the back of my mind, behind me, in a sense.

James and John were paired together because the two areas they represented were closely related. The same personal weakness that led me to attack the James character before thinking through the situation made me vulnerable to the John character.

I couldn't confront the dream characters with anger—my battle with James taught me it wouldn't help. Instead I listened for them and watched my life for their influence. They could take any form, but behind the masks they felt the same. I knew it was them by our inner dialogues.

To resolve the situation with the James character I studied the ways of the noble warrior and absorbed the lesson of never striking out in anger. To resolve the situation with John, I looked at attractive women and controlled the reaction of my sex drive, proving to myself that I would not be manipulated by passions. I questioned the characters about who they were and why they were in my dream and gained insight into what they represented inside me. After a while I knew them well. They could pop in anytime, anywhere, and attempt to take over my agenda. A dialogue with John under those circumstances might go like this:

Me: I hear you, John. I saw the hot chick too, and I heard what you said about trying to pick her up. Come out from the background of my thoughts and stand in front of me.

John: Then why don't you say something to her, Mr. Big Talk? You'll never get laid if you don't try.

Me: I'm in a grocery store, not a nightclub, and she looks more interested in what's for dinner than in going home with me. Besides, I don't know her.

John: That's no excuse. You're afraid to go after what you want.

Me: I get nervous when I try to pick up women. You are correct in that sense. It's just not the right time.

John: You won't get many more notches in your belt that way, and I know you keep track of how much pussy you've had. How long has it been since you've gotten some? Too long.

Me: You know a lot about me, John. Thanks for pointing that out; it makes me more determined to do things right.

John: Putz.

Me: At least I'm not a pimp wannabe like you'd have me be.

In my early days of using active imagination, I wrote out the dialogues, but after while they became less structured and more spontaneous. Any character that makes a strong impression or recurs in your dreams becomes fodder for active imagination. What is most important for making it work, other than the right attitude, is finding or creating an environment of peace and quiet to talk with yourself. Without it, the characters aren't heard, their presence isn't felt, their voices can't be distinguished from background chatter, and the experience makes no real impression. However, once you gain experience and insight and establish lines of communication with your dream characters, your dialogues can occur anytime, anywhere, leading to insights about yourself you might never gain otherwise.

Using Symbols

A concrete and easy way of making your dreams part of your daily life is to make the symbols part of your person and environment. Two examples have been given already—the wolf and the frog. The wolf came to me in a dream and became a tattoo on my shoulder. When I awoke, I bought a poster of a gorgeous wolf to put on my bedroom wall. Every time I saw it I was reminded of the dream and what it means. If you recall, the frog symbolized the dreamer's shy, sensitive inner nature that needed to be protected. I suggested she place a figurine of a frog in her living environment or wear a T-shirt with a frog on it to remind her of the dream and its message.

I used to wear an Egyptian cross necklace as a symbol of taking the beliefs I inherited from my culture and making them my own, prompted by my dreams to forge a personal spirituality rather than just reject what I learned from certain Christian churches. I associate the Egyptian cross with gnosticism, which to me means faith acquired through knowledge, not belief. Wearing that symbol reminds me I've found a spirituality that arises from my personal experience, not from the teachings of someone else. It connects me with my dreams and enriches my daily life.

I have dreamed of eating certain foods and in waking life benefited from eating more of them. I've dreamed of activities like playing basketball that I made part of my exercise habits. I have dreamed of visiting places and followed up by visiting them in waking life. I have dreamed of friends and family members and took it as a sign to call or see them. Often, those people have been thinking about me recently, too, and when I get them on the phone, the reaction is, "Wow, I was just thinking about you and wondering how you are doing."

Of course, not every dream symbol is a direct suggestion for waking life. I shared a dream my partner Lisa had where a friend from graduate school she hadn't seen in a decade was in her car holding a map. The dream was not a prompt to get in touch with her old friend, but a reminder that he had taught her something that would help her "map out" how to achieve a goal.

Your imagination is a potent tool for living your dreams. Use it in ways that feel right and do not adversely affect you or the people around you. Your dreams provide a great variety of images to creatively use. The techniques described here will get you started.

Tip

Look through your dream journal and list the symbols that recur or stick out to you. Each one is charged with potential energy, energy that can be felt or intuited in the dream. By connecting yourself to the symbols, you release that energy into your daily life. List all of the symbols if you want to, instead of just the ones that stick out, and look for possible meanings in dream dictionaries or websites like dreammoods.com. And always remember to look for ways of making your dream symbols a concrete part of your daily life.

Controlling Dreams, aka Lucid Dreaming

Once you wrap your mind around the meaning behind your dreams and how to apply those lessons in your daily life, you might be ready for graduate work: dream control. This technique is popularly known as "lucid dreaming"—becoming aware that you are dreaming while in a dream. Once you know you're dreaming, you have the option of consciously following along with the story as if watching a movie, or controlling what happens next. Want to learn what it's like to fly under your own power? That's what a lot of people do when they first experience lucid dreaming. Want to make love with a fantasy mate? That's another popular choice.

Before giving you some tips for how to become lucid and control your dreams, I want to emphasize that this is advanced dream work and should only be undertaken after the basics of dreaming and dream interpretation have been mastered. Your unconscious mind gets limited opportunities to speak, and it will insist on its time, preventing or hindering lucid dreaming until you are ready. Some people treat lucid dreaming like a sport or a conquest, and I warn you it is nothing to fool with. You wouldn't climb Mount Everest until you were well prepared or else you are asking for trouble.

Having said that, there is nothing innately dangerous about controlling your dreams. As one person said to me, once you know you can drive your dreams wherever you want, you can't help but want to take them for a spin. Question is, how do you recognize that you are dreaming while in a dream? The most popular method I have found is the "reality check." To determine if you are dreaming, ask yourself if the scene you see is reality or a dream. Make a habit of it while awake so that you will also make a habit of it while you are asleep. Some people look at their hands and count their fingers. Some look at a clock and try to notice time discrepancies. Some reach for something they always keep in their pockets, like a special coin, a key, or a pocket knife.

The best way to become aware that you are dreaming, though, is simply to recognize the landscape of your dreams. This becomes easier as you work with them. I've known people who tried to be lucid while dreaming before they even regularly remembered their dreams, and inevitably they did not succeed. Like mountain climbing, learning to lucid dream is a process of learning and mastering new skills.

I became lucid for the first time after a few years of dream work, an experience I describe in the inner dialogue section on page 126. By becoming aware that I was in a dream, I was able to ask the right question before the dream ended. I didn't do a reality check, but at the time I was reading a book about lucid dreaming, and I think that helped me. What seems to work best is simply training your mind to recognize you are dreaming by any means that feels right to you.

Another way of training your mind to lucid dream is by playing video games, discussed more in Part II, "A User's Guide to Dream Symbolism," on page 193.

The lucid dreaming community at Reddit has links to many resources related to lucid dreaming, and experienced lucid dreamers hang out there who will gladly answer your questions. Join them at http://reddit.com/r/luciddreaming to learn more about the subject.

✳✳✳

These three steps are enough to get you started remembering, interpreting, and living your dreams. If you are new to dream interpretation it might be wise to save the rest of the book until you have remembered and interpreted a few dreams, to allow time to digest and apply what you have learned so far. However, more material is waiting for you in the coming pages that will expand your knowledge. You don't have to take it in all at once; dream interpretation is a long journey, and most important is to learn to walk on your own by the end. If what my dreams have told me is correct, at the end of our lives we recede back into our dreams, and we all live again to continue the dream of life.

PART II

A User's Guide to Dream Symbolism

This section is by no means a complete guide to dream symbolism or dream symbols. That is a book in itself. Instead I want to cover some related subjects that either haven't been mentioned in the main body of the book or were only touched on briefly. Also, I want to show you how to interpret symbolism, rather than providing static definitions. Once you know how it works, you can interpret any dream symbolism yourself.

Drop by my blog, Dreams123.net, for more information and resources. Use the search box and you'll find explanations of everything from the symbolism behind colors like blue and red to lively discussions of what lions, dogs, or spiders can mean in your dreams.

Make It Personal

You are about to discover a trove of dream symbolism, and somewhere in there will be reminders of your dreams. When that happens, stop reading for a moment and write down any insights you gain in your journal. Then go back and decode your dreams.

For example, you are about to learn that one of the interpretations for flying is "taking off" or "soaring" in your personal life. If this reminds you of your dreams about flying, use the information to understand the rest of the dream. If the dream is about a plane overloaded with luggage and is too heavy to reach altitude, it might be saying that baggage in your personal life is (or was) weighing you down. If the plane veers off course, look for ways your life path changed around the time of the dream. If the plane is delayed, ask if an important decision was delayed, or your life delayed in some way.

Do this exercise and the others suggested in this book and you will fill your personal treasure chest with insights about your dreams.

Archetypes

The concept of archetypes was introduced to the modern world by Carl Jung, who developed it while trying to answer what connected the motifs and imagery that appeared in his patients' dreams and other people of vastly different cultures and backgrounds. The patterns he recognized led him to identifying and categorizing a wide variety of collectively inherited ideas, images, and thought patterns known now as archetypes.

Robert Moore, a student of Jung's work, further refined Jung's concept in his groundbreaking book coauthored with mythologist Douglas Gillette, *King, Magician, Warrior, Lover: Rediscovering the Archetypes of the Mature Masculine.* I learned how to recognize archetypes in dreams from what I learned in it, and I recommend it to everyone who wants to know more about the subject. While the book is written from the perspective of the male psyche, it is enlightening about archetypes in general. Moore identifies four primary archetypes in the human psyche: the Monarch (King or Queen), Magician, Warrior, and Lover, each explained briefly next.

The Monarch archetype is a pattern hardwired in the mind for the leader in all of us. While historical and mythological figures can appear in dreams representing this archetype, I find modern leaders like Bill Gates, Steve Jobs, and Hillary Clinton filling the role more often these days. The Monarch in your dreams might take the form of a lesser known person like a coach you know, a teacher you've had, or a relative who embodies leadership characteristics. This archetype has a vision for your life and sets forces in motion to achieve it.

The Magician archetype dominates the areas of intellect and skill. The medical field, science, advertising, engineering, and the arts, among others, require a lot of what you might call a certain kind of magic: the ability to apply knowledge, refine skills, and manipulate energy. In dreams, this archetype can take the form of magicians from popular stories, illusionists like David Copperfield, or people who display unusual abilities, especially psychic abilities. This archetype has the ability to make things happen in your mental life.

The Warrior archetype makes things happen in the physical world. The force that drives you to work, practice, or study hard comes from this archetype. The Monarch inside you might want you to get a promotion at work, but it's the Warrior who compels you to get there early, or to put in the extra time at work, sports practice, or your hobby. The Warrior is connected with your discipline and your ability to protect your space. Mythological figures in dreams can represent this archetype, but more often I encounter modern-day warriors like Chuck Liddell, Chuck Norris, and Buffy the Vampire Slayer.

The Lover archetype provides the motivation and inspiration for everyone to create his or her own little kingdom, a life filled with connectedness, good relations, and, of course, love. The Lover brings an appreciation for fun and art. It makes the Warrior take vacations, the Monarch act with compassion, and the Magician come down from the ivory tower. It compels us to find romantic partners and experience intimacy. It urges us to connect with the world, each other, and ourselves.

Another archetype mentioned in this book is the Divine Child. As Moore sees it, the Divine Child is the early version of the Monarch archetype, the first archetype to usually emerge in a young child. It is a source of enthusiasm and zest for life. When you feel excited at new beginnings or just happy to be alive, that's the Divine Child at work in your life.

Finally, a God archetype is mentioned here, too. It arises from a universal need to give meaning to life and comprehend our existence.

Each of these archetypes has an early version and a mature version, and each version has a shadow side, so this subject can get complex. For our purposes I'm going to keep the discussion simple and encourage you to read Moore's books if you want to go into more depth.

The simplest way to think of archetypes is as patterning forces that give shape to human energy, structures in a sublayer of the mind that affect everything on the surface. Archetypes are analogous to magnetic force, which is invisible, but its influence can be seen physically on objects that respond to magnetism. For example, dump a handful of iron filings on a piece of paper and then run a magnet underneath. The filings will line up like soldiers in formation, following the lines of magnetic force. Archetypes similarly influence thoughts, feelings, and behavior, and appear in dreams mostly as characters, but sometimes as settings or other symbolism. You don't have to know archetypes to interpret dreams, but understanding the basics can be helpful.

Archetypes are made from opposite energies bound together; therefore they often appear as opposite characters, explained in the section "Dream Pairs" (page 33). One pole is called the "positive" pole and the other is called the "negative" pole, describing the "charge" of the energy centers, like the polarity of electricity. Things get out of balance when one side of the archetype is dominant over the other. Another characteristic of imbalanced archetypal influence is the person bounces back and forth between the two poles, also known as bipolar. The goal is to achieve balance between opposites.

Next up are two dreams showing archetypes at work.

Exposed in Open Court

I'm in a courtroom with four rectangular tables arranged as a square in the middle. One of the tables is blocked by a curtain, but I know it's there. A trial is about to begin, and my parents are seated with the observers. An aggressive man appears from behind the curtain and begins talking harshly to an abused girl in the back eating needles.

The arrangement of the tables immediately jumps out at me. The square configuration symbolizes the four primary archetypes.

The court setting indicates something wrong has happened and someone stands accused. It is where truth is revealed.

The presence of the dreamer's parents points to the original source of the conflict, though they are not on trial, just there as a clue.

The curtain hides something from the dreamer: an area of herself out of view and in need of her attention. Then the man appears from behind the curtain, and his connection to the girl eating needles is exposed, his identity revealed. Judging by his and the girl's behaviors, I see the shadow side of the Warrior archetype. The shadow of that archetype manifests sadistic or masochistic energy, sometimes shifting between the opposites, and here is a prime example. The sadist, knowing he is about to be "exposed in open court," tries to shift attention to his counterpart, the masochist in the back of the courtroom eating needles. The abuser blames the abused, and the abused believes she is somehow responsible. She takes it out on herself by eating needles, symbolizing self-inflicted damage to her body and self-image. The pairing of these two characters shows how their opposite natures are really two sides of the same coin, symbolizing an archetype at work in the dreamer's life.

With the knowledge imparted by this dream, the dreamer can recognize patterns that are hindering life progress, recognize forces at work deep in the psyche, and learn to use them consciously to end the internal conflict. Every sadist needs a masochist to tango, and by recognizing both sides as originating internally, the dreamer can rise above the conflict and no longer feed into the shadow side of the Warrior archetype.

The Maiden and the Matron

I am at the mall looking for work outfits, and I see myself in a mirror in the center of a store. The mirror is shaped like a pyramid with four sides. I can't see myself clearly, and my Blackberry distracts me. Then I see a young girl and an old matron behind me in the mirror. The young girl snatches my Blackberry and starts pressing buttons. "This toy is no fun!" she fumes. I expect the matron to return my phone—I am aghast at the thought of the girl pressing the wrong button and emailing personal photos to my work colleagues, or something else which might be very embarrassing—but she appears not to notice. "Aren't you going to do something?" I demand. The matron slumps over, withering before my eyes, and says, "If only I'd taken better care of myself when I was your age."

Stores are places where we make buying decisions, so they can act as terrific metaphors for any choices made in life. Choosing a job can be compared to shopping in a mall, with multiple stores (employers or careers) to pick from, followed by a purchase (an investment of time and personal resources in return for money and benefits). The dreamer is thinking through identity issues related to work life. She could be considering a promotion or a different position, symbolized by wrapping herself in new clothing, but she has a hard time seeing what the change might "look" like. She can't "see" herself in the new role.

The mirror's position in the center of the store indicates it is reflecting something central to the dreamer's life, and its shape as a pyramid is a dead giveaway of its archetypal origins. The dreamer sees a young girl and an old matron in the mirror. Here the dream shows the archetypal roots behind her inability to really "see" herself in a new work role, depicted as the Maiden–Crone archetype. It shows the source of the dreamer's reluctance to take on more work responsibility.

Part of the dreamer relates to the young girl more interested in play than work. The girl—the active or "positive" pole of the archetype—snatches the Blackberry away from the dreamer, and her reaction ("this toy is no fun!") is a clear opinion of what a young side of the dreamer thinks about the device and its importance in her busy adult life.

The matron is the passive or "negative" pole of the archetype. She symbolizes the fear of growing old. Frustrated, the dreamer expects the matron to intervene—getting involved in the conflict of the opposites rather than rising above—and is worried about the girl embarrassing her. This reaction can be interpreted as the dreamer fearing that the immature part of herself that hates the demands of her job is going to someday nuke her career. The matron represents another hindrance to the dreamer taking on a harder job: the fear it will make her old before her time. The matron's last words as she slumps over express this fear.

Tip

The archetypes are often depicted in your dreams in images that are divine, royal, magical, or mythical.

Body

The settings of dreams or the features in those settings sometimes symbolize your body. Settings can speak to your body's health, well-being, and development, as well as to what it feels like to live inside your body, its needs, or its perceptions about body image. Symbols for the body include settings such as buildings, landmarks, or vehicles, or landscape features like hills or trees, but sometimes the body is depicted directly. Grocery stores, restaurants, hospitals, doctor's offices, and gyms can be used for communicating information about the body and its needs.

Dreams can sometimes give symbols for specific areas of the body. For example, a waterslide can symbolize a throat, a fluid pump can symbolize a heart, and a balloon can symbolize a lung. Locations within dream settings give clues to the areas of the body illustrated. A roof or top floor can indicate the head area. The bowels can be symbolized by a basement or plumbing. Tributaries of a river or branches of a tree can represent arms or legs.

I interpreted a dream that symbolized a uterus and female sex organs as a four-sided building with an enclosed courtyard and underground tunnel leading into it. What really gave away the meaning was the parking attendant that required the dreamer to put hot sauce on her tongue in order to enter the courtyard. The hot sauce symbolized a LEEP (loop electrosurgical excision procedure) where precancerous cells are burned off the cervix, something that the dreamer had experienced. The soft, moist flesh of the tongue is used as a symbol for the dreamer's cervix.

Dreams can relate areas of the body to specific areas of life. For example, a dream about being shot in the leg or foot might relate to something that hinders your ability to move life forward. A wound on the arm or hand can symbolize something that hinders your ability to take action or work. The throat can symbolize your ability to speak your mind, and the face can symbolize your public persona or personal character, since faces are closely associated with identity.

Here are a few areas of the body and some ideas about what they might symbolize:

- Feet: a foundation; movement in your life; willingness

- Legs: ability to make progress; "legs to stand on"

- Hips: balance; openness; destiny

- Stomach: "gut" instincts; digestion; where anxieties or fears are felt

- Back: something unseen, unaware, or behind you; burdens; responsibilities

- Chest: pride; accomplishment; power; guilt

- Heart: compassion; love; hate; envy

- Arms: work; strength; self-defense; separation

- Wrist: need for action; connection; flexibility (applies to all joints)

- Hands: turning thought into action; having a grip on something, as in "get a grip;" making money; unity

- Neck: speech; articulation; connection between the mind and body and between the head and heart
- Eyes: "seeing" something; looking at a subject or area of life; the window to the soul
- Head: thinking processes; sense of direction
- Hair: thoughts; instincts; personality
- Teeth have their own entry in this section

In dreams involving the body, I frequently find references to its care and health. Here is a dream with a message about the body's health.

Saving a Dying Fish

I walk into a room in my house and see two dead fish in a fishbowl, and a third fish is barely alive. Something is wrong with the water— it's yellow. At the bottom of the bowl are chunks of fresh cucumber. I need an algaecide to clear the water, so I call my friend, who turns out to be nearby in the kitchen. He goes to the cupboard and eats something like red Jell-O, and I get frustrated because he is not help-ing me save the fish.

The symbol that makes the connection with the body is the fishbowl. It reminds me of a bladder or kidney, and I suspect the yellow water indicates something out of balance, sickly, probably related to the urinary system. Seen this way, the cucumber makes sense because drinking water with cucumber chunks is a folk remedy for urinary issues. The dreamer reported feeling like she might have a urinary tract infection. Her friend's action of eat-ing red Jell-O seems absurd, but in the dream he acts out what is really needed: ingestion of something that cleanses the body. The setting inside the house combined with the symbolism of the fish bowl says to me that the dream is taking a look inside the body.

The health of the body is a top priority for dreams, alongside the health of mind and spirit. Threats to health are often seen ahead of time and brought to life. Take this example:

I grab a soft drink from the refrigerator in the kitchen, drink from it, and feel something strange in my mouth. I freak out when I reach in and pull out a black spider and realize I've already swallowed others.

The kitchen setting relates to dietary choices, used in this case to warn graphically against drinking too many sugary, acidic beverages, which in quantity are venomous like spiders to the liver and digestive system.

Other dreams speak more to body image and perception than specifically to health, though dreams layer meaning on top of meaning, like this.

Bridget Jones Marathon at the Gym

I'm at the gym on the elliptical machine, like usual, and for some reason all of the TVs are showing a Bridget Jones movie marathon. One of the fitness trainers walks by and remarks that Gentlemen Prefer Blondes *is on the TV in the free weight area. He then remarks that Marilyn Monroe's favorite exercise was shoulder presses with dumbbells.*

When at the gym during waking life, the dreamer avoids the room with the dumbbells because she fears bulking up her muscles. In the dream, the gym setting is used to tell a story about her motivation for exercising. The *Gentleman Prefer Blondes* reference relates to this female's perception that men prefer scrawny women. So she spends all of her workout time on the elliptical machines, symbolized by the Bridget Jones movie marathon. But her body wants a balanced exercise routine, and her dream chooses to deliver the message via a trainer.

Monroe, an icon of feminine beauty, used dumbbells as a regular part of her exercise routine, and no one complained about her being overly muscled. The dreamer knows this fact about Monroe though doesn't apply it to herself, and the dream uses it to layer the story with meaning. The gym tells a story about her current exercise regime and how to improve it, while dealing with the underlying perceptions that drove her to focus on weight loss over strength training.

Books

Life is compared to a river flowing forward day by day. The unconscious mind, however, sees life like a book already written. To the unconscious, everything that happens is supposed to happen, so books in dreams can take on high importance, containing vital information about a dreamer's past, present, and future.

Of course, books can have a simpler purpose related to everyday life. For example, you might work on an issue or question and that night dream of reading about a solution in a textbook. The information is already in your mind; you just need some help connecting the dots. I've known dreams to speak more directly by referring to the page of a book where you'll find the solution to something on your mind, but generally the unconscious mind speaks with hints and clues.

Books, then, are used to communicate both everyday information and once-in-a-lifetime information to the dreamer. The difference will be felt or intuited. If the dream setting is a school and you're at a desk with a math book open, you're likely dreaming about a learning process related to math, or your feelings about the subject. Or you might be trying to "add up" something in your life by weighing options, or even processing something that happened in a math class that day. But if the dream setting is a tower in an ancient castle and the book is a leather-bound tome, you're probably dreaming of something much more significant.

Really significant dreams feature books that contain important information about your life. When you take the opportunities to read about your life described from another point of view, you'll likely be floored by its accuracy and objectivity. Your dreams can describe your innermost self in ways you can't consciously put into words.

In many religious traditions, including Christianity, there is a Book of Life that records everything a person does and thinks. Edgar Cayce refers to this as the akashic records. Whatever term is used, the concept is universal. The words in a Book of Life are really descriptions of how a person's consciousness affects his or her environment, the imprints left by having your feet planted in this reality. In that sense, a book is a great symbol for a life.

When books appear in your dreams, pay attention to how they are used and the importance given to them. Since books in dreams symbolize knowledge you already have, you have it whether you know it or not. Just keep in mind that the unconscious mind won't reveal its secrets until you are ready, because dreams only act in your best interests, and you are ready when you have mostly figured things out on your own.

Children and Pregnancy

The majority of dreams that use children and pregnancy as symbols have nothing to do with having a child or getting pregnant. It is said that a person can be pregnant with ideas or possibilities, or give birth to a creation, so dreams frequently compare creativity and endeavors to children and pregnancy. It is certainly one of the first interpretations to consider if the dreamer does not have children in waking life, or if the children in a dream are unfamiliar.

If you have children and dream about them, you might be working through issues or feelings related to raising them, or picking up clues to their needs, health, or emotional lives. Parents with young children report a recurring theme of small animals in their dreams, symbolizing their small children. In a dream we looked at previously, a mother dreamed that children disappeared from her daughter's day care and the adults didn't notice, an obvious warning that something is wrong when mom isn't around (page 56). Another mom dreamed that a pill had fallen under her couch where her baby might find it (page 113). Dreams give valuable information like this about raising and protecting children.

This next dream uses pregnancy to address a related issue.

Giving Up My Baby

I am pregnant but it doesn't show in my belly. I give birth alone to a little baby, and my only thought is a massive fear that I won't be able to keep the child because I have to be back at work the next day, and there is no way my employer will give me maternity leave. So I put the baby in a white carrier bag and leave it in a bin behind the place where I work. I check the next day and the carrier bag is tied shut. I presume the baby is dead.

An important personal detail to note about the dreamer is she is early childbearing age. What I see in this dream is fear that she won't be able to have a child because her work schedule won't allow it. She isn't actively trying to get pregnant, but she won't even consider it in her present work situation. Putting the baby in a carrier bag behind her workplace is a way of storing the hope until the time is right.

Another way to interpret the dream is the dreamer is pregnant with creative energy but has no outlet for it; her job takes too much of her time and energy. Putting the baby in the carrier bag would then represent saving her creative energy for when she has an opportunity to use it. However, the pregnancy never shows in her belly, and the reason why pregnancy works as a metaphor for creativity is it grows inside the dreamer until birthed. Plus the dreamer's reaction of thinking about getting time off of work is a clue that it is a related issue.

Whichever interpretation of pregnancy fits the last dream, neither one confirms the dreamer's worst fear of what it might mean: that she was some kind of heartless baby killer. No, what she sees in the dream is entirely symbolic. A dream like this can be a prompt to think about preparations that can be made for pregnancy, like getting in shape, or finding the right father or work situation.

Often to their bewilderment, men can also dream of being pregnant and giving birth. This dream was mentioned previously:

I'm a straight male, but I dream of being in a hospital and giving birth. The child isn't mine; it belongs to a male friend of mine who delivers it.

To understand what giving birth means to this dreamer, I had to know his associations with the friend in the dream. He described the guy as hardworking and successful. So giving birth symbolizes the qualities of the friend that rubbed off on the dreamer. He decided to work harder so that he could be more successful like his friend.

Of course, keeping in mind that dreams do speak literally sometimes, dreams about pregnancy or giving birth can be signs that the dreamer really is pregnant. I've read dozens of reports from women who dreamed about being pregnant before they consciously knew it. Some women have correctly dreamed about the gender of their baby, even dreamed of what to name them. These dreams often show the dreamer together with someone she knows who has children—mothers and sisters are commonly chosen—making preparations of some kind, like shopping for baby clothes or toys, or decorating a baby's room.

I mentioned a dream earlier about an addict in recovery who meets his future daughter, and she tells him if he doesn't stay clean, she'll never be born. I interpreted this dream as a literal warning to the addict. If you know you have a soul, it's not hard to imagine that it existed before you were born, and if you existed before you were born, you might have helped make the arrangements for your life's circumstances. It's an idea supported by dreams. Of course, the unborn daughter can represent a side of the dreamer that will never emerge if he continues his addiction, but I see nothing else in the dream or the dreamer's comments to support that conclusion. The message, in his case, is literal.

Children in dreams can also represent a younger or less mature part of you. Aging is seen by dreams as the addition of layers, with the previous layers still alive and active underneath, going all the way back to birth. What you might call the first layer is referred to as the Divine Child archetype. In dreams it takes form as an infant that inspires joy and awe at life, sometimes with a glow of innocence or holiness around it. Other layers are what you might call your inner children.

The child's needs can tell you which stage of development is symbolized in a dream. Young children need comfort and assurance. Older children need guidance and close attention. Young teens need challenges, independence, and security, while older teens need freedom and opportunities. When these needs arise in daily life, dreams point out where they originate. For an example of this, let's take a look at this next dream.

My boyfriend and I are on a beach, and a three-year-old girl that is supposed to be my daughter is with us (I don't have children). I ask him to keep an eye on her as I go off and do something with my mom. When I see my boyfriend later, my daughter isn't with him, and he says he left her at the skating rink.

The daughter is a surrogate for a young part of the dreamer that depends on her boyfriend to watch out for her basic needs, like comfort and assurance. That the dreamer's boyfriend is trusted to care for the daughter in the dream says a lot about her trust in him with her needs. But when he leaves the daughter at the skating rink, this shows that he isn't as attentive as he could be. The dreamer's child is actually an inner child.

Colors

The simplest way to understand the symbolic use of color in dreams is to think of it as "coloring" the dream. Color explains subtlety of mood, thought, perception, and feeling. It paints the picture. Colors used in dreams explain themselves by their hues. To discern what a hue means to you, ask yourself what it reminds you of and how it makes you feel.

Any time a color sticks out, describe it in a few words. For example, the color blue to me is calm, thoughtful, and "deep." With those associations in mind, I next think about how the color is used in a dream and combine it with other symbolism or actions. A blue room, for example, might symbolize the place in my mind where I ponder or analyze.

Color is also used to show connection between elements of a dream. Coming up, we'll see a dreamer who plays a blue guitar while wearing a blue shirt, showing that the symbolism of the guitar and the character are connected ("Playing Guitar in a Hotel Lobby," page 202).

Since colors are used in many figures of speech like "seeing red" and "green with envy," also look for wordplay when a color is prominent in a dream.

Note: Some people don't dream in color. However, their dreams can make references to colors, and knowing the symbolism can help with understanding the references.

Red

"Seeing red" is a common expression used to symbolize an angry state of mind. But red isn't always an angry color. At its most essential, red represents the essence of life, the color of blood, basic human energy.

Red is the color of the first chakra, the energy center at the base of the spine. Chakras are connected with the endocrine system. They are centers in the body where basic human energy is given shape and definition. I learned about chakras from practicing yoga and reading about Edgar Cayce, and I mention them here because I find that color in dreams can relate to certain chakras.

The color red and the first chakra are related to the basics of life: health, protection, self-preservation, aggression. Without these, the other colors of life have no foundation to paint upon. You can't be a deep blue thinker if no red blood is pumping. The meaning can be literal, as in blood in the veins, or figurative, as in "hot-blooded." Zest and passion for life can be described as having "rich blood" or "blood coursing through the veins." Red, then, can symbolize life force or passion as well as anger. To know which, look at how it is used in the dream.

In a dream discussed earlier, the dreamer looks for a solution to save a fish dying in a fishbowl, and calls a friend for help (see page 144). He appears on the scene and eats red Jell-O, which appears to be completely unrelated to solving her problem, but the Jell-O symbolizes something that cleanses the body, and red symbolizes essential nourishment. In a dream about an apocalypse (see page 94), the planet turns red like blood, signifying a situation related to the dreamer's aggression.

Orange

Dreams that use orange are often related to the dreamer's sex life, reproduction, or fertility, as we saw in the dream "Walking the Platform" when the dreamer tries on an orange sweater that doesn't fit (see page 14). It is the color of the second chakra, centered in the hips. Someone I know had many dreams with objects and scenery colored orange during a time when she was trying to get pregnant.

More examples are: opening an orange door, which is from a dream about entering a new area of sex life; taking off in an orange plane, which is what finding an enthusiastic lover can feel like; and juggling oranges, a dream image illustrating the complexity of maintaining or "juggling" several sexual relationships at the same time. The pumpkin is a classic symbol of sexuality or sex-related themes.

But keep in mind also that an orange is a fruit and can represent healthy eating, not sex. The color orange in dreams is associated generally with the drive to create, which includes fertility and sexuality but also creativity in general. As usual, the action tells the story.

Yellow

Yellow is associated physically with the solar plexus, the location of the third chakra, related to willpower and drive. The solar shade of yellow shines in dreams with vitality; however, a lack of vitality shows up as a weak hue. During lethargic depressions, dreams can be cast in pale yellow, sometimes in institutional settings where the dreamer is controlled by impersonal authorities. The association with yellow and cowardliness—for example, a man is described as "yellow" if he won't fight—is common. Filmmakers use yellow-colored lenses to convey a sense of lethargy, or the opposite sense with a brighter hue, implying the energy one can gain from a sunny day.

Times when I exert greater than normal effort, I dream almost nightly of playing tennis. The yellow tennis balls glow particularly bright, and now I see the connection between the game, the color, and my ability to exert energy and hit the targets I set for my life.

Optimistic people are often described as being "sunny," recognizing that the yellow of the sun is loaded with cheerful energy. The connection extends to yellow foods like bananas, which are used by athletes to provide maximum energy with the lowest volume. When I was more involved in sports, I often dreamed of eating bananas. If yellow features prominently in a dream, pay attention to the hue and ask if it reminds you of anything.

Green

Think of the saying "green with envy." Why green? Well, it is the color of the heart chakra, also called the fourth chakra, and envy is the heart's desire to satisfy itself by possessing what someone else has. No wonder then that green is the color of money! But there are many shades of green, and many ways it can be used in dreams and language to express meaning.

In general, earthy shades of green communicate connection with nature, growth, life. I remember dreaming of a green, grassy field that represented new possibilities in my personal growth. During my twenties, at an age when sexuality and mating were forefront in mind, carrots with bushy green tops frequently appeared in my dreams. Baffling at the time, the symbolic meaning is obvious to me now. Above the ground a carrot grows a green top, and below the ground it grows an orange root. Which is a lot like mating: On the surface, choosing a mate and maintaining the relationship is a green growth of the heart's desire. Below the surface, mating is about sex and reproduction. The sex drive springs from the second chakra, represented by the color orange. And you don't have to watch a lot of nature shows to know that the shape of the penis for many species is shaped like a carrot.

Green also comes in emerald varieties, which I've found to be a good sign in dreams, showing the heart moving closer to something it wants. However, I know examples of hues of green that are too intense and have sickly tones, which is a sign of envy, dark desire, or the heart overpowering the head. There are also moldy shades of green that can imply decay, and neon green that demands attention. These are some of the many meanings that dreams can give to the color green. Like all symbolism, it must be put interpreted in context.

Blue

The color blue brings to mind deep thoughts, reflection, and sometimes melancholy or depression described as "feeling blue" or being in a "blue mood." It has strong associations with mood and emotion, but also with thought and insight. When associated with chakras, blue is divided into two shades: light blue (the fifth chakra) and indigo (the sixth chakra). The fifth chakra is centered in the throat and is linked with communication and self-expression. The sixth chakra is centered in the forehead and is linked with the "third eye" and alertness.

In "Swimming with Dolphins" (see page 47), the dreamer describes her symbolic immersion in the clear blue water as exhilarating. She might have had a completely different impression if the water was brown or red.

Blue, like all colors, can appear anywhere in a dream, and it is there purposefully. For instance, if a colleague appears to me in a dream wearing a drab blue-gray T-shirt beneath a sunny yellow jacket, I might wonder if she is secretly "blue" beneath her sunny optimism. If the shade of blue looks more like a cloudless summer sky, I might wonder if she has a rich mental life covered by a more genial or driven personality.

Violet

Violet is called the royal color in part because it is associated with the "crown," or seventh, chakra located at the top of the head. It symbolizes connection to Spirit and the higher mind. Kings and queens dress in the royal color and wear crowns to show their divine connection and right to rule. Which is not to say that if you dream of wearing a purple robe, you are actually royalty! Each of us, though, has an archetype inside that serves the purpose of ordering and leading our lives, providing leadership, direction, and inspiration. Dressed in violet, perhaps wearing a crown or sitting behind a big desk, the Monarch archetype identifies itself to the dreamer sometimes through obvious symbolism, sometimes obscurely.

For example, an author dreams that his kitchen is in disarray. The surfaces are cluttered and nothing is put away where it is supposed to be. A chef character wearing a chef's hat refuses to work until the kitchen is cleaned, and the dreamer promises to take care of it. The chef then hurries off to order eggplant.

The kitchen setting is a work environment, and in the dreamer's waking life his work area is a mess. He's allowed his writing desk to become cluttered with a hundred little things that need to be put away or addressed, and the deeply creative part of himself is unable to work through the distractions.

To understand the chef character, think about what chefs do: plan a menu, prepare ingredients, combine them, cook it all up, and prepare it for service. This is a fantastic metaphor for crafting a novel: an initial idea leads to notes and research, thinking through character and plot details, writing, editing, and finally publishing. It's an enormous labor of love that, when successful, serves up some hot 'n' tasty literature.

The chef's significance as a character from the dreamer's unconscious mind is illustrated by the chef's hat, which is a sort of crown, and another detail: The eggplant's deep purple hue provides a clue that the author's "inner chef" is preparing to work on a new book, and the inspiration for it comes from the dreamer's highest mental source, the seventh chakra. That is where the chef's order for eggplant is received in the mind. Eggplant symbolizes the author's new book.

Sometimes details as seemingly insignificant as eggplant give away deep meaning; but don't get sidetracked or bogged down analyzing every detail to death. It is more important to follow how a dream feels and what it says directly. In the last example, the connection is obvious to the author because his writing desk is like a messy kitchen. Whether or not the dreamer understands the meaning right away, the call to action—to clean the kitchen so Chef can work—rings loud and clear. The dreamer agrees to clean the kitchen without having to be convinced, because something inside him knows it is a distraction. This goes to show that the actions of the day are thought through and prepared for at night, during dreams.

White

Interestingly, white light is achieved when all colors of light—red, green, and blue—are reflected, while white pigment is without any color. In dreams I have seen white signify purity, desolation, or a lack of distinction. Characters dressed in white often announce themselves as beneficial to the dreamer, connected spiritually, even holy. White landscapes and settings, however, I've found to often be sterile, a sign of something seriously lacking in the dreamer's life (unless the landscape is white with holy light). Snowy or frozen desolation is the most frequent theme I've encountered in dreams about deep depression. Lack of color is a dream's way of pointing out the need for more vitality or liveliness.

White can also represent something that is indistinct, like in the dream "Disappearing White Figure at the Front Door" (page 206). The figure doesn't represent an actual person or even a part of the dreamer; it represents a nagging feeling trying to get his attention.

In "The Snowstorm" (see page 54), a white horse signals that the unconscious has sent a means for the dreamer to escape a period of depression, symbolized by the snowstorm. Two meanings symbolized by one color.

Black

Black light absorbs all colors, and as such it has all sorts of possible meanings when it appears in dreams. Most commonly I find that it symbolizes mystery or the unknown, but it is also frequently associated with a person's shadow side (see page 38).

Two characters colored black in my dreams symbolize two very different parts of myself. In the first dream, I batted against a voodoo baseball pitcher, his skin very black and his body covered by animal fur and feathers. He threw a wicked pitch that corkscrewed past my swing. I turned to the umpire for help, but he just sort of shrugged. In that dream a shadowy part of myself came to life that originated with a late childhood experience dealing with how unfair the adult world can be. *That's right, people aren't always fair,* my young mind had to grapple with, *and sometimes they take what is rightly yours and ain't no one going to help you get it back.* The voodoo pitcher throwing corkscrew pitches that defied the laws of physics shows up in my dreams when I am dealing with feelings of being treated unfairly.

In a second dream, I talked with Barack Obama about politics. I sensed his authority and followed his instructions because he is the president. Obama in that dream symbolized my Monarch archetype.

Black can also mean "unknown" or "mysterious" because of the blackness of outer space and the black of night. Both are places of mystery. "Blackened" is a term ripe with possibility to describe explosive or hot situations in life. Being "in the black" means your business is profitable, while a "black operation" can mean covert activities. And finally, black is associated with death.

Death

Death dreams are usually distressing, and can even make you wonder if the reaper is coming. But dreaming of death has a variety of interpretations, and only one involves physical death. To interpret death in a dream, look beyond literal definitions. For example, have you ever felt you could die from embarrassment? Or have you had an opportunity die on the vine?

I say death dreams are *usually* distressing because some are about accepting it, and are actually meant to reduce distress. Someday your heart will stop beating, that's a fact, so of course your dreams are going to try to prepare you. When you can accept death in a dream, you are empowered to live life more fully or pass away more easily.

Stories are commonly heard about dreams warning against imminent danger in waking life, so it's natural to wonder if a dream about death or tragedy is prophetic. The answer is no, most likely. A guy once nervously asked me about a dream where he died in a plane crash. He was scheduled to take a flight the next morning and wondered if he should cancel it. I thought the plane crash symbolized something related to a fear of flying or feelings about his personal life "crashing." I don't know if he took the flight, but I checked the news and no commercial flights crashed on the day he was scheduled to fly. Unless there are further clues that a dream is a literal warning, like if the plane or flight number matches with reality, it should be interpreted as being symbolic.

Death in dreams can symbolize loss or the end of something, for example, the end of a relationship, someone's influence, or a phase of life. I have known college students to dream of a parent dying because that is what it feels like to leave the nest. Relationships that drift apart can feel like a little death, especially when they involve someone you were once very close to. Here is a dream that illustrates the comparison:

A friend calls and tells me that my ex-boyfriend from high school has died. I feel sorry for him, but I realize I don't really feel anything romantically for him anymore.

A relationship that ends is said to "die," and feelings that linger are said to "die slowly." The dreamer's ex-boyfriend is not about to literally die, but her feelings for him finally have. She is totally over him.

I interpreted a dream about a mother hanging herself as involving a threat that could eventually kill the relationship between mother and son ("Mom Hanged During Apocalypse," page 94). The dreamer was involved in illegal drugs, and his dream warned him that their relationship was changing for the worse. In the dream "The Deadly Pageant" (page 60), the dreamer's father is dead at first, then comes back to life as a way of saying that the dreamer's sister, by having sex before marriage, was doing something he taught them to avoid.

Sometimes we go through changes that can be compared to death in a sense of the word. The transition from childhood to adulthood involves the "passing away" of immature parts of oneself. A hard-partying college student might dream of dying when entering the professional world because restrictions on time and opportunity mean the party animal has to die—or it might refuse to die, causing a conflict with work. When parts of ourselves are visualized dying off, it can be, and often is, a good sign. Out with the old, and in with the new!

Dreams about animals dying are sometimes related to parts of yourself that have a kinship with the animal and are threatened with dying off or receding back into your unconscious mind. This dream uses that symbolism:

I am at a hotel pool and find three kittens in the water that appear to be dead. I notice one is still alive and try to save it.

Kittens are viewed by this dreamer as innocent and playful, so with those associations we have a clue to what the dream is about: the "death" of something innocent or playful in himself. The hotel setting suggests that he is in transition, changing. The pool is symbolic of his unconscious mind. Everything above the waterline is said to be conscious; everything below is unconscious. From talking with him I gather that he is a teenager under a lot of stress to conform to his peer group. Being innocent and playful in that crowd will only get him picked on and taken advantage of, so he forces those traits into hiding—they go "underwater." In a sense, they die off. However, his reaction of trying to save one of the kittens shows that he isn't ready to let go of all those parts of himself. He could have reacted by letting the last kitten drown, which would symbolize forcefully making anything innocent or playful about himself go away, but he didn't.

The symbolic interpretations of death should be considered first, but sometimes dreams about death are about actual death. Just before Abe Lincoln was assassinated, he dreamed about seeing himself in a casket, dead, in the White House. Boxer Sugar Ray Robinson dreamed before a fight that he accidentally killed his opponent. He wanted to back out of the fight but was convinced it was "only a dream." He accidentally killed the guy.

Dreams with literal interpretations are much less common than dreams with symbolic interpretations, and to know the difference, you begin by eliminating the symbolic ones. If I was the person called to counsel Sugar Ray about his dream, I'd begin by asking him if he felt like he wanted to kill his opponent, even in the sense of "God, I could kill that guy!" Was there bad blood between them? Or did he fear that killing an opponent was a possibility? In which case, the dream can be interpreted as bringing up a fear to confront it. He might hesitate to "go in for the kill," making him a less effective boxer.

Ruling out those interpretations, I'd ask if the phrase "make a killing" felt connected to the dream. Robinson could be working through thoughts about how much money he was going to make if he won the fight or lost it.

I'd also ask if he saw himself in the other boxer and was, in a sense, fighting with himself in the dream. People react strongly to qualities in others that are similar to their own shadow sides. There could be a deeply personal reason behind the dream tied to Robinson's perceptions about himself and his opponent.

But we know how this story ends. If I rolled through all possibilities and nothing rang a bell, I'd have to tell Robinson to consider the literal interpretation.

It is also common to dream about loved ones who have passed away. The purpose is to grieve and process the loss. Sometimes, though, these dreams can facilitate contact with loved ones in the next life by working through personal issues first, then opening lines of communication. The continuation of consciousness after physical death is accepted as fact in the dream world, and in my experience it is true, but the interpretation of a death dream is tricky when strong emotions like grief are involved. Dreams are known to fulfill wishes, and if something is wished for strongly, like the wish to see a deceased loved one again, it is likely to pop up in some form while dreaming. Only after ruling out other interpretations should the interpretation of actual contact between souls be considered. If you'd like to know more about this, check out Elsie Sechrist's book *Dreams: Your Magic Mirror.* It has great insights and thoroughly documented cases of contact between the living and the dead.

As you can see from these examples, death in dreams is most likely a symbolic representation, not an actual warning. The difference is intuited by making associations with aspects of the dream: settings, characters, symbols, actions, and your feelings and reactions.

Tip

There is nothing to fear even if a dream foretells death, but there is probably something in your waking life that needs attention.

Drugs

Following the rule to always consider the obvious, doing drugs in a dream can symbolize something about the dreamer's drug use. However, people who have never done recreational drugs might dream about it. It's a discrepancy that screams "symbolism!" Even for people who regularly use recreational drugs, their drug-related dreams are still often symbolic.

To figure out the symbolism, think about the common perceptions of what drugs do. Drugs are known to change a person in a bad way. They're addictive. They're used to escape reality. They're something we are told not to do.

They're also a catalyst for having new experiences, and this meaning is used frequently in dreams. In this sense, doing drugs in dreams is a way of telling a story about new experiences, new ways of looking at the world, new perspectives of who you are. You take LSD or mushrooms or whatever, and suddenly the world looks very different. The experience is comparable to anything that alters your view of reality.

As with all symbolism, the action tells the story. For example, if you dream about taking LSD and the next thing you know you are on a spaceship exploring the universe, you have a strong sign that new experience or discovery is the theme of the dream. However, if you do the drug and suddenly find yourself in a sewer or surrounded by threatening dream characters, you have a sign that the dream is about consequences or perceptions.

Of course, drug users will dream about their habits or addictions. Many of those dreams involve purchasing or handling the drug. In one dream looked at earlier, purchasing cannabis was compared to buying fruit from Mexicans in the desert (see page 94). Dreams can also illustrate what it feels like to use drugs, or their impact on daily life: emotions, feelings, finances, living situation, relationships, and self-image. Using drugs can feel like a roller coaster or hot air balloon ride. People addicted to drugs or alcohol commonly dream of monsters, affected family members, cops, and bad situations which can't be stopped. An addiction can be a real monster, and cops can represent forces trying to stop it, forces originating inside or outside of the dreamer.

Flying and Falling

Whether flying in a craft or under your own power in a dream, the symbolism is probably related to going somewhere in your life. You have a destination to reach, a goal in mind, a flight to take. You want to "go somewhere" or test yourself, or perhaps you want to experience something that exhilarates you. The action defines the meaning.

An exhilarating takeoff might mean your life is taking off. A new opportunity, job, or relationship can make you feel this way.

Sex and other thrills can also feel like flying or taking off. Flying a plane is like navigating your life, especially your mental life, because thoughts are said to "soar" and intellect is associated with the "upper realm." Landing a plane might describe bringing something to a conclusion, or bringing high-flying ideas "down to earth." Turning a plane (or other flying craft) in another direction could symbolize taking your life in another direction. Jumping from it might symbolize abandoning plans or getting detoured.

Flying under your own power in a dream can be related to testing yourself and what you are capable of, and feeling confident. Superheroes fly; they are not limited by mortal constraints, and flying can be associated with defying limits or getting around obstacles. Keep in mind though that the higher you fly, the more you must be grounded. Also, flying in a dream can be a story about detachment or getting away. Flying in general is associated with a sense of freedom and wide open possibilities where "the sky is the limit."

Falling, however, has connotations of a life that is not going where you want it to go. I had dreams of falling, until one night I hit the ground hard, representing "hitting bottom" in my personal life. I see this symbolic use pretty often. Falling can also be a metaphor for "the bottom falling out from under you." A spouse suddenly separates and you feel like your life is in free fall. A layoff notice at work sends you into a tailspin. The figures of speech used to describe these circumstances really hit the mark when it comes to describing what they feel like. Phrases like "falling in love" describe a different feeling of falling as ego boundaries fall, and in dreams the imagery is used to vividly describe what the person is experiencing. Your feelings will tell you more than anything what the imagery means in your dreams.

Former Partners

Dreams about former partners can mean that old, unresolved issues are ready to be resolved, and something in the present triggers a reminder. So if the ex was a mooch or a cheater and you find yourself in the same situation again with a new partner, your dreams connect the past with the present by dreaming about the former partner when really you are thinking about the new person in your life. It's not to say that the present situation is identical, but it can *feel* like the past is being repeated. Dreams show how the present connects with the past and how to avoid repeating mistakes.

I see this function enacted a lot in people who were cheated on. Soon after getting involved in a new relationship months or years later, they dream about the ex. They start to feel close with the new partner, hesitate out of fear of being cheated on again, and dream about it through a past reference.

The next dream combines a current relationship with a former partner in a way that is unmistakable once you know how to interpret dreams:

It's my wedding day and everyone I know is present. I'm about to walk down the aisle when my ex-fiancé barges through the doors and says he is there to rescue me.

Holy cow, isn't it obvious the dreamer wants to be rescued from making a huge mistake? She really is about to get married when she has this dream, and to dream of her ex barging in to "rescue" her is an unmistakable message. She knows she is about to marry the wrong guy. Maybe her heart is still with her ex, or she wants a relationship like they had and knows she won't get it with the guy she is about to marry.

The next dream also involves a former love.

Cutting Ties with My Ex

I'm in a restaurant and my ex appears across the table from me. I walk into a side room stacked to the top with boxes of olive oil, televisions, and toys. I want to take some olive oil, but a waitress tells me I can't. I walk back into the dining area. My ex is now seated with another male working together on a contract. I'm told things are being worked out. I go back to our old house and look around to see if there is anything I want, and there isn't, so I leave.

A lot can be left behind in past relationships—sometimes material possessions, but also possessions of the heart and mind. I think these are symbolized by the olive oil, televisions, and toys stacked up in the adjoining room of the restaurant. The action of going through and looking for stuff to keep is comparable to leaving a relationship but bringing the things you want to take with you. For example, some couples spend a significant amount of time watching television shows together, and the activity becomes central to the relationship. After the relationship ends, those shows act as a reminder of the ex. If the dreamer had wanted to take a television with her in the dream, it might mean she still watched some of the same shows or had sentimental feelings she wasn't ready to leave behind.

The toys could represent a point of view on relationships that is "childish," and leaving them behind means leaving behind that way of thinking. Or the dreamer could be "toying" with an idea or a new approach to romantic relationships. The olive oil symbolizes something about the relationship she wants to keep but can't, perhaps related to diet or Italian heritage.

The contract her ex works on and the message that "things are being worked out" are signs she can put the relationship to rest for good. Meeting in a restaurant across a table from an ex is this dream's way of saying the dreamer is choosing to negotiate an end to the relationship's influence on her.

Former partners appear in dreams to work through present issues in relationships, either directly like the dreamer rescued on her wedding day, or indirectly like the dreamer who hadn't seen her ex in years, then dreams that everything is being worked out. Dreams almost always pull material from the last day or two, so if you dream of an ex, connect it with the present. Does something about your current partner remind you of your ex? Are you working through old feelings? Do you have regrets? Is it hard to let go? Are you ready to try again, or do you hesitate because something feels unresolved? These are the sorts of questions to ask yourself.

Tip

Dream characters that are former romantic partners can also stand in for a detail about the old relationship, so look at that time of your life for clues to the meaning. For example, say you dated someone long ago when you worked together in the Peace Corps and that person appears in your dreams. If there is nothing about the relationship that feels unresolved or connected to your current situation, you might look at what the Peace Corp represents. It might mean that you miss the sense of purpose you had, the idealism, the commitment, or even the opportunity to live abroad.

Marriage

In dreams, marriage can symbolize the "marriage" or union of the conscious mind with its counterpart, the unconscious—sometimes called the "marriage of the soul." If the terminology bothers you, just think of it as a union between parts of the psyche. It is the result of a long process of bringing the two sides closer, and seems to be the deepest reason for dreaming. In fact, dreams about holy union or marriage are known to be common for people who have advanced to the final stage of work with their anima or animus.

While dreaming serves biological, physiological, and neuro-logical purposes, the main purpose is psychological: to prepare a wedding between the conscious side of the mind and the uncon-scious side by first conducting nightly marriage counseling ses-sions. But look at the action before drawing that conclusion. If the marriage is with a dream character that reminds you of your anima or animus, it backs the idea of union in the psyche. If the marriage is to someone you despise, the dream says something else entirely. A dream that tells the story of an arranged mar-riage between the dreamer and a Mafia guy ("Mafia Slave," page 208) shows how a psychological complex takes root. The dream marriage in this case is something you wouldn't wish on your worst enemy.

For people thinking about or planning a marriage, dreams of marriage are likely to be about working through related issues, thoughts, or feelings. Earlier we looked at a dream centering on a bride about to walk down the aisle when her ex-fiancé barges in at the last second to "rescue" her—which has nothing to do with spiritual union, and everything to do with preventing a bad mistake. In that case the dream speaks to a marriage decision, not a symbolic bond.

Part of the holographic function of dreams is to run lifelike simulations (or dress rehearsals) and ask "what if?" Dreams ask: "Would you really be happy married to this person or that type of person? Would it work? Is this what you really want?"

Of course, if you are married you can learn about your spouse and your relationship through your dreams.

Expand the idea of marriage and more possibilities come into play. Some people are said to be "married" to their jobs, express-ing the idea that anything requiring a big commitment can be described as marriage. Also, think of the humorous possibilities. If you dream of walking down the aisle with your pet, I'd bet in some way you feel married to it—especially if the pet sleeps in your bed!

In a dream mentioned previously about marriage that is both humorous and meaningful, a female dreams that the television host Rachel Maddow proposes to her on live television (page 32). Marriage in that case symbolizes making commitments to social causes.

Ocean and Water

Long before humans began to comprehend the immensity of the universe, we had the ocean to help describe something huge, mysterious, and powerful. Dreams use oceans to describe the unconscious mind, which is also huge, mysterious, and powerful. By comparison, the individual is a boat floating atop a massive body of water, an ego on the surface of a mind with endless depth. Jungian dream-based therapy is sometimes called depth psychology for this reason.

Dreams use the analogy of a boat compared to the ocean to describe the relationship between the conscious and unconscious sides of the mind. Dreams of calm seas and smooth sailing can describe a good relationship between the two sides. Choppy seas or sinking ships, on the other hand, are signs of trouble. I've analyzed dreams about the ocean rising up and flooding the coast, a sign that the unconscious and its reservoir of memory and emotion are pouring into waking life. I've had dreams of the ocean receding that symbolize my consciousness expanding and claiming "land" that had once been "underwater," meaning unconscious. A pier is similar symbolism because it can describe how your consciousness reaches into the unconscious mind, into the depths of who and what you are as a person, to bring new parts of yourself "to the surface."

If you dream of the ocean, ask if a comparison is being made to how you feel, or to something going on in your life. Take note of the water, if it's deep or shallow, calm or choppy, clear or murky; these details can describe feelings or the nuances of a relationship, for example. Also, look for figures of speech like "coming up for air" or "wind in your sails."

Water in dreams can refer to the unconscious, but before jumping to conclusions, pay attention to the context and action. If the water is boiling hot, the dream might not be referring to the unconscious mind but instead to a metaphor for being "in hot water" or "boiling mad." On the other hand, people at ease will dream of a pleasant bath or a nice swim, a gentle and con trolled exploration of their inner depths. The analogy comparing water to self-exploration is used in the dream "Swimming with Dolphins," page 47.

The seashore or beach is where the conscious and unconscious sides of the mind meet, often symbolizing that information from the unconscious mind is being communicated in a dream.

Water in dreams can also symbolize emotions or feelings, as in "watery emotions," so ask yourself if the water in your dream is comparable to something you felt the day or two before it, paying close attention to the action.

Overwhelming emotions can be compared to a flood. In a dream about a volcanic eruption symbolizing bottled anger let loose (page 93), the water that rushes in afterward symbolizes cooling hot emotions. A squirt gun can be a symbol for emotions that are childish or projected. Being drenched with water in a dream can express what it feels like to have someone's feelings "dumped" on you, or strong emotions "rain down."

Water can also represent the "water of life" that is drunk through personal or spiritual development—especially if the water flows from a spring or fountain, or is delivered in a special way, like poured from a vessel held by a priest or goddess.

And always bear in mind that dreams can be literal; there is the possibility that water in a dream can symbolize the need for hydration, bathing, or cleansing of something like negative emotions or ego inflation.

Rape

Rape as a dream theme pops up a lot in young females, but it can appear in anyone's dreams regardless of age or gender. To understand the symbolism, think of other definitions of the word "rape." In one sense, to be raped is to be humiliated. In a dream I helped interpret, a female at a gas station is raped by a man she encountered the previous day ("Raped at a Gas Station," page 77). We didn't need to know anything about the symbolism of a gas station, because it was an actual setting where an event took place: While filling her gas tank, she encountered a guy who hit on her in a real sleazy way. It was humiliating, and her dream enacted the feeling by comparing it to rape.

In another sense, to be raped is to be overpowered. I hear the term used in sports and video games to describe when one competitor thoroughly beats another. "Raped" is also used in the sense of "raping the planet," a metaphor for taking advantage of something or someone in selfish and destructive ways.

Rape and sexually tinged violence can express feelings the dreamer has about being forced, used, or coerced. Externally the coercion might be from a relationship with an abuser, or with someone like a spouse, parent, or situation that controls them. Internally, the coercion stems from ways we can make ourselves conform, or force down parts of ourselves that are unwanted or rejected. Anything forced on us can feel this way. However, the force isn't always overt; sometimes we voluntarily make ourselves into something we wouldn't be otherwise, because we are rewarded for doing so. Women who use their sex appeal manipulatively, or who conform to cultural standards of femininity at the expense of living out their full potential, can dream about violence and rape as a way of symbolically expressing how they feel deep inside. Men will ignore their personal needs and work themselves to death trying to provide for their families, pursue some ambition, or live up to an idea of what a "real man" is, and their dreams can present the situation as themselves or a projection of themselves being raped.

For someone who has actually been raped, dreaming of the attacker(s) is a way of reprocessing the event. If the dreamer can overcome the fear and act in self-defense, it's a way of subconsciously dealing with it.

Relationships

Relationships stir people at the deepest levels, especially romantic relationships, and dreams are bound to follow. Dreams about relationships usually involve traveling somewhere together in a vehicle, staying somewhere together, doing something together, or meeting up. In these dreams the actions and symbolism tell a story about the relationship—where it is headed, the dreamer's feelings, the true nature of the person of interest, social perceptions and assessments—every area of relationships that can be examined. Here is an example:

I take my new boyfriend to meet my friends at a nice restaurant, and when he talks, I notice some of his front teeth are missing. I'm caught totally off guard and feel like I might die from embarrassment. My boyfriend really has all his teeth—I've checked!

The restaurant setting announces itself as a dream about choices, and for this dreamer her choice of boyfriend is on her mind. The presence of her friends says, in a sense, that the dreamer wonders if he will fit in. The missing teeth speak to social status; someone missing front teeth probably can't afford dental care, and it gives the impression of low social status.

While teeth in dreams can have many meanings (page 191), the dreamer's reaction is most telling: She's embarrassed. When she says that she has checked her new boyfriend's teeth, what she means is he appears to be of a certain background, breeding, and appearance that meet her expectations. But add her friends and their opinions to the equation, and he no longer measures up. The dream is either expressing a fear that he won't be accepted by her friends or that she's noticed something disagreeable about him but ignored it. Or maybe, since teeth can be related to things spoken, the missing teeth symbolize that her boyfriend says things that won't go over well with her friends. Whatever the case, it's a sign of trouble for the relationship.

Dreams have other ways of describing dim prospects for a relationship:

I'm out on a small lake in a rowboat and my girlfriend is nearby in a similar boat. My boat springs a leak so I climb into hers and row away. A guy on shore is selling balloons. I buy some balloons and give them to my girlfriend.

The action of climbing out of his rowboat and into his girlfriend's boat says to me that the dreamer's life might have been sinking when he started the relationship with his girlfriend. Since *his* boat has the leak in the dream, I assume it has something to do with his life around the time he started the new relationship. At first I think it could mean he left another relationship just before the current one, but there is no one in his original boat with him, no ex-girlfriend at all in the dream, so it's possible the action of sinking is related to a "sinking feeling" that the current relationship will not go far, or that his life has "sprung a leak," or something similar.

The balloons also tell the story of the prospects for his current relationship, and they're not good. Helium balloons are kept aloft by artificial inflation, and as the gas goes out of them, they sink, just as the air or buoyancy can drain from a relationship. The action of giving balloons to his girlfriend says that he unconsciously recognizes the inevitable.

If a love interest is the subject of a dream, you can bet that your mind is exploring your feelings or rating your possibilities— even giving advice on how to proceed. I've known dreams to say very directly, "this person has an interest in you" even when the dreamer is unaware of any attraction. Maybe the person was giving off a vibe and you missed it; or, dwell on someone hard enough and you might sense the intense thoughts and dream about it. I've also known dreams to say, "this person has no interest in you." I'm using the romantic definition of relationship, but the same process of interpretation applies to any interaction with familiar people in dreams: family, friends, coworkers, anyone you know.

This next dream tells a story about a college student's prospects for a new romantic relationship.

I walk past a friend of mine in the library. In waking life, I'm confused about whether or not she actually likes me. I accidentally enter the girl's bathroom. I take off my pants, exposing my penis, quickly realize I'm not in the men's room, pull up my pants, and walk out calmly. People start freaking out. I go into the men's bathroom and hear girls chastising me. Several follow me into the men's room as I wash my hands. I scold them and say it was an accident and they're overreacting. The last girl is a nice person I know. She comes in and says, "I have a question about your friend" (the one I'm attracted to and saw in the library), and I scream at her to get out and not come back, along with everyone else.

The dream announces what it is about in the opening scene: the dreamer's relationship with a friend, a romantic interest. A library is a place to get information, and he questions what his friend's real interest is, so he goes to the library to find out. At first I see a connection to the dreamer's self-perceptions when he enters the women's restroom and drops his pants. I interpret this action as expressing anxiety about sexual prowess; a central concern among guys his age is if they "measure up." Maybe the uncertainty with the friend is making him question his desirability. Maybe he is feeling exposed because he has expressed interest but she hasn't.

The girls that follow the dreamer into the men's room chastising him give voice to something nagging him. Originally the dreamer reported that he washed his "pants" in the men's room, not his "hands," then corrected himself. At first I thought it might be a Freudian slip, since washing pants can symbolize washing away negative self-perceptions related to that area of the body. But to "wash your hands" of something means to be done with it, finished.

Relating that idea back to the beginning of the dream, I think the dreamer feels that his relationship with the friend in the library is not worth the trouble it causes him, and he wants to "wash his hands" of her, but his feelings are public and his schoolmates are involved. This interpretation is reinforced by his angry reaction to the girls following him, symbolizing rumors and gossip, and especially by his reaction to the nice girl who tries to ask him a question about his friend.

The dreamer's hostility toward the nice girl reveals hostility toward the subject of the dream. He shared during the interpretation that he had been feeling fed up with the immaturity of the dating scene, the gossip and head games. My guess is that pursuing a relationship with the original girl isn't worth the hassle, but he ought to give the nice girl in the bathroom a closer look. His dream chose her for a reason, perhaps to say she might make a better dating partner.

Dreams with positive signs for a relationship show the dreamer together with the person having a good time, interacting naturally. The good feelings that accompany these dreams are indications of chemistry, but don't jump the gun. Ask your dreams for clarification if you continually dream about someone. It's a sign that he or she strikes a chord in you some way, but it's not always the romantic way.

Sex

For those of you who have read or skipped this far to get to the sex dreams, you are about to be disappointed. I don't have graphic examples—except one, and it doesn't end the way you might expect. In fact, sex in dreams quite often describes something other than sex.

With some dreams, it's true, what you see is what you get. Dream sex can express the desire for a real-life encounter with the person dreamed about, or just in general. If the sex partner is unfamiliar, ask if the dream character reminds you of anyone. Use of surrogate characters is a way to allow dreams to progress without interference from the ego, which might otherwise alter the dream with its objections or desires. Sex with random strangers or even with people we know can be a way of asking "what if?" as in the case of this next dream.

I'm at a party and a girl I know from class pushes me back into the bathroom and onto the toilet. She takes my hand and places it on her woman parts as she pulls off my pants and underpants. I'm about to penetrate her with my erection when my psychology teacher barges in and asks us what we're doing. We run away to an area with bathroom stalls, and my mom is in one of them. Then I wake up. I'm not even attracted to this girl.

The young male, a high school student, has probably daydreamed about scenarios with sexually aggressive females. What would he do in real life if it came true? He says he isn't attracted to the girl in the dream, but his erection says otherwise, bringing the scenario down to earth—he isn't likely to bang his fantasy girl at a party, but a hookup with someone from his school is possible. It's a way of asking "what if?"

The dreamer's reaction gives the answer: In real life he would have second thoughts. The psychology teacher's entrance just as he is about to have hot random sex says to me that the dreamer struggles with the "psychology" of sex. The dream points to the source: his mother. I bet she has told him sex with strangers is dirty or wrong. In the dream she is in a bathroom stall, and he is on a toilet when about to have sex. Both clues point to a perception of sex as "dirty."

Then there is the dreamer's use of the term "woman parts" instead of just saying pussy or vagina. His phrasing brings to mind someone who has heard and talked about a lot more sex than he has experienced, a high school kid who wouldn't know what to do with a girl who came onto him like in his dream. The dream tries to help him realize the source of the psychological issue and work through it in a lifelike simulation, so if he ever does get lucky like that, he won't be interrupted by thinking about his mom!

Sex is often a metaphor for anything intimately experienced. For example, musicians might say performing is "better than sex" or "like the best sex"; similarly, listening to music that is intensely enjoyable is comparable to the music made between the sheets. Recall the dream about the DJ and the slow music (page 43). I wonder if the dancing and kissing in the dream metaphorically describe the dreamer's relationship with music, or her feelings related to experiencing it in her body. Dancing, with its rhythm and coordinated movement, is like sex and sometimes a precursor to it, and music sets the tempo. Slowing the music down could be a way of saying the dreamer might enjoy her music and her sex more if she slows it down.

Music and the arts evoke responses that feel sexual, as do exhilarating ideas and experiences. Take this example:

My professor and I ride on a big magic carpet, flying over cities, seas, and mountains. He is very sure of himself, amazing in how he commands the carpet to fly places for me to view. Then he lays me down on the carpet and we make love. He ejaculates a small seed into me. Near dawn he drops me off on my dorm roof. He then flies away, saying "see you in class." He is a great professor, but I'm not physically attracted to him at all, so why did I dream of making love with him?

The sex here symbolizes how the professor wraps the dreamer's mind around the subject of study. The magic carpet symbolizes how his lectures take the dreamer's mind to places she hasn't been before, to view the world from his perspective and "magically" understand it new ways. The professor is not attractive to the dreamer physically, but mentally he stimulates her, and the experience is comparable in some way to making love, keeping in mind that dreams exaggerate to make a point and be memorable. The seed he ejaculates is the knowledge he implants through his dynamic lectures, which grows in the dreamer.

Dreams address any areas of life that need it, and sex is no exception. Dreams can give advice about how to conceive, orgasm, ask for and get what you want, feel comfortable, or choose a lover—any aspect of sex life or reproduction. Sex dreams that appear to be just about the experience of sex, no metaphor, are likely to be explorations of sexuality. Enjoy them and learn, paying close attention to your reactions and what they say about you.

Symbols for sex and the corresponding body parts appear in dreams, though not as frequently as Sigmund Freud led us to believe. Every rolling field doesn't symbolize the curve of a hip.

Every grain silo doesn't symbolize an erection. Look for more clues to verify the interpretation.

I know of dreams that used lotus flowers and tulips to symbolize the vagina. I also know of a dream a guy had about plowing a field with his penis, a play on the sexual metaphor "plow a field," expressing the dreamer's desire for more field plowing during his daily life! Phallic symbols are everywhere—towers, rockets, flag poles, etc.—however, I can only think of one time in the last ten years when I've found a phallic symbol in a dream that actually symbolized the male sex organ. Unless a dream has a reason to talk obliquely about a sex subject through symbols, there is just no point. A direct message is more likely to grab the attention of, and be understood by, the dreamer.

In the dream that used a phallic symbol to represent the real thing, a male high school student found pubic hair on a hotdog he was eating. He had recently come out as gay and began having sex with men, and eating a hotdog with public hair on it was his dream's way of making a comparison.

If you are not sure what a symbol means, ask how you respond to it and how it makes you feel. Feelings of arousal and desire are pretty easy to spot unless they are repressed, in which case they are likely to be expressed symbolically in dreams so that the dreamer can respond without interference from the ego.

Dreams can show sexual dependence or immaturity. These dreams come in all varieties and sometimes involve the dreamer trying to have sex with someone (or something) who doesn't want to. Or the sex is absurd or obscene. These types of dreams illustrate fears like rejection, or misconceptions about sexuality, and are essentially healthy ways of working through issues. Sometimes, though, they show that the dreamer's internal wires are crossed. Sexual dependence often begins as the ego imposing a sexual relationship on anima or animus, the representatives of the unconscious side of the mind, which isn't supposed to happen. The object of desire is seen in a dream and the dreamer reacts by wanting sex, preventing other actions from taking place—like an actor that tosses out the script and wings it during a live performance. It causes the dream to veer off in another direction.

Someone who's been made to feel guilty about sex, or who is deeply repressed, will sometimes have vivid sex dreams, which at the root are compensation for the extremes of his or her conscious mind. Unfortunately for people who don't understand dreams, they might believe sex dreams are temptations to be avoided. Even nuns and priests sworn to celibacy and virgins dream of sex. Whatever the case, if it can be enjoyed, I think it is a way for the unconscious mind to compensate for what is missing in waking life, or identify what is wanted from a sexual relationship, or prepare for the future.

Cheating

Another frequent sex-related subject is "cheating"—having sex in a dream with someone other than one's significant other. Bottom line: It's not cheating. The dream might represent unconscious wish fulfillment, or it might arise from a sex vibe picked up off the person dreamed about (if he or she is familiar), but it's not comparable to cheating. If the dream sex is pursued in spite of other commitments, it might be asking "what if?"—an attempt to make the dreamer aware of buried feelings or a new perspective emerging. Cheating is sometimes a matter of opportunity, and if the unconscious mind sees trouble ahead, it will try to warn the conscious mind.

Cheating has several potential meanings. One meaning of cheating is "breaking the rules," and relationships can have all sorts of unwritten (and written!) rules. For example, a dreamer came to me asking why her husband dreamed about her cheating on him. I suggested that in some way he felt she was breaking a rule or expectation of the relationship, or that he was jealous of the attention she gave other men. That interpretation rang a bell: Her husband was jealous of her talking with other men, and his dreams pictured his feelings as her cheating on him.

Another dreamer asked me why she dreamed her boyfriend was cheating on her. She felt confident that he wasn't actually seeing another woman and couldn't understand why she would have cheating dreams. I suggested that she might feel he was breaking a rule of the relationship, or "playing unfair" in some way. She responded to that idea because her boyfriend would do things like have guys-only nights out and not invite her, even though she liked to do guy things like watch sports and drink beer. To her, being excluded was "cheating" because she felt she followed "the rules" but he didn't. These are a few of many ways cheating can be used as a metaphor.

Shapes

Shapes can give context and structure to the stories in dreams. For instance, you dream of talking with a group of friends about a really exciting idea you can accomplish together, and someone suggests ordering a pizza. Surprisingly, your fifth-grade teacher delivers it, the one who told you time and again that to reach your full potential, you have to study and work hard. The pizza with its round shape is actually a sign that the unconscious mind is trying to deliver important information, because round objects can represent fulfilling potential or becoming complete as a person. The dream's message is that the teacher's advice needs to be taken seriously, or else the exciting idea will not become a reality.

Shapes of buildings and the arrangement of objects are deliberate symbolism used by dreams to tell the deeper story. Pay particular attention when an object is shaped differently than usual, like a square airplane or a triangular door. Incongruous dream details that differ from waking reality are places to really ask questions about what is going on and why.

Let's explore some possible meanings of different shapes as used in dreams, keeping in mind what is most important: what shapes symbolize for you and how your dreams use them to tell the story.

Squares

We live in a four-sided world—four directions, four elements, four states of matter—and squares are the most obvious way for dreams to represent the "construction" of your life and the world around you. Squares can show up as settings like rooms or buildings, also as objects and arrangements, and can be used by dreams to illustrate how the dreamer fits into her environment.

Squares are related to establishing or maintaining yourself in the physical world, and to internal arrangements between parts of your mind, particularly between archetypes. In math, squared means multiplying a number by itself, which has possibilities if used symbolically. In figures of speech, square can be slang for someone who doesn't know how to have fun, or avoids excitement or risk.

When squares appear in your dreams, look for ways that your life is described, analogies for how you live, and how your life is "constructed" like a house. Because the four sides of a square are balanced, dreams that feature squares can be about achieving a balanced life or state of mind.

Rectangles

Rectangles are also four-sided—essentially squares with two long sides and two short ones—and can symbolize relationships or situations that are out of balance. For instance, an exaggerated rectangle like a long hallway that grows longer as the dreamer travels through it is a way to describe anything that gets longer or more difficult after it has begun, or a goal that gets further out of reach. If you dream of being seated at one end of a long table and your significant other is at the opposite end, it can be a dream's way of saying you are far apart emotionally, or the relationship is out of balance, or both.

When rectangles appear in your dreams and feel important to the meaning, look for something in your life that needs balance. (See "Exposed in Open Court," page 139). For instance, if you are a strongly logical person, ask how your feelings can inform your values, or if values based on your feelings are shunned. Conversely, if you are a feelings-oriented person, maybe you need to balance it with more logic and reason. Or if you are a highly intuitive person, ask if you give "shortened" attention to factual, sensory information. Valuing one way of processing the world at the expense of others causes imbalance in the psyche.

Because rectangles are so common in the everyday world, look for ways they are used in dreams to show exaggeration or imbalance. For instance, a doorway that is shortened can symbolize low expectations of the future, or figuratively stooping to a lower level.

Triangles

Nothing says "power" in a dream better than a triangle or pyramid. Power, at its most essential, is the energy that drives humans to do the simplest or most complex actions. Triangles and pyramids can tell stories about how you use energy or power—or don't. It's like a peek under the hood of the car that is you, to gain knowledge about what drives you, motivates you, compels you, and makes your engine go.

The root of triangle and pyramid symbolism is the tremendous clash of opposite energies that forms the foundation of consciousness. The more this dynamic energy is mastered, the more a person becomes conscious and rises above the conflict. That is symbolized as the top of the triangle and the all-seeing eye.

Dreams can use triangles and pyramids to tell stories that promote becoming more conscious of your motivations and what you are made of deep inside. Internal balance is the goal.

In "The Maiden and the Matron," (page 140), a mirror shaped like a pyramid is used to show the dreamer an archetype at work in her life as she is considering a new job and what it will require of her.

When triangles or pyramids appear in your dreams, ask yourself what areas of life need more energy or power, and which are already "charged up." If conflict is involved, do you rise above it? What, if anything, keeps you down? What does the dream say about what you want and what you work at?

Circles

If you think about what "hitting the bull's-eye" means both literally and figuratively, you get an idea of how dreams can use circles as symbols. Circles and round objects in dreams can be a sign that a person is headed in the right direction in life, or at least working toward it, because circles generally speak to your personal growth—the drive to become whole and complete as a person, expressed in the phrase "to come full circle." In my dreams, circles often appear as balls—baseballs, basketballs, tennis balls—and the actions reveal the meaning.

For example, back during my college newspaper days, I covered the men's basketball team, coached by one of the best, Bob Huggins. Night after night Huggins appeared in my dreams because I responded to his demanding style. During that time of life I was developing the part of myself that can work intensely, and my dreaming mind found an example to learn from. When working my hardest in a way that would make Coach proud, I'd dream of swishing fantastic shots on the basketball court. To this day, when "missing the mark" in my personal life, I dream of missing my jump shots or losing my dribble.

All around us are circles: the sun, the planet, the moon—and inside us too are round cells composed of atoms shaped like circles. So there are many good reasons for circles to appear in dreams, and behind them all is guidance from the inside toward becoming a complete person. In this sense, circles are soulful. See "Dance of My Soul," page 217, for a dream that uses this symbolism.

Remember the dream about finding a round amulet in the snow during a raging storm (page 54)? Knowing that snowy landscapes can represent depression and that storms are common metaphors for internal conflict, I interpreted the talisman as a sign that the dreamer would soon find her way through the turmoil represented by the storm, which was the case.

Sometimes a dream produces only a reference to a circle. For example, if I dream I'm given a job with the Knights of the Round Table, my rational mind might balk: "That's only a legend!" However, knowing that dreams speak through references to other things, I'd be wise to learn more about the Knights of the Round Table who sought the Holy Grail, and ask if it connects somehow to my life. The quest to find the Grail is a metaphor for searching for meaning and something worthy to serve. To get the message across, my dream doesn't have to arrange the knights around a circular table. It's not saying, "move to England and search the countryside for chivalrous knights," but search within my life for honor and heroism, serving the forces of good encountered along the way.

When your dreams use circles or round objects, try associating them with anything in your life that has come full circle or is evolving toward it. Ask if the circle symbolizes something you are trying to improve or a target you are trying to reach. Pay close attention to how a circle or any shape is used by a dream. If the circle is a ball, what do you do with it, and what is the result? If it is a circular spaceship, where are you trying to get to, or where are you being taken? Also consider whether a dream uses a circle to tell you that you are going in circles.

Technology (Gizmos, Social Media)

Technology is changing the way we communicate, interact, and get information, and it is changing our dreams, too. Not only are gizmos and social media showing up in dreams, but today's abbreviation of language and ideas through texting and Twitter is affecting the way dreams tell their stories. Dreams have always spoken in a sort of shorthand, symbolic language. Now it appears to be getting even shorter for people who are plugged in with technology all day. People who have grown up immersed in this digital world expect to get their information in quick hits, 140 characters or fewer, so the dream coach has to be brief.

Social media also bring us into contact with people we haven't actually seen in years. Next thing we know we are getting status updates about what the person had for dinner, or who he or she is dating. These tidbits of information influence dreams, especially if we check social media feeds just before bed. Here is one such dream:

Just before going to bed I checked Facebook and saw that my ex-boyfriend has a new boyfriend. So then I dream that I am supposed to go out and meet my ex and his new boyfriend, but I don't put much time into my appearance and think I look shabby. I

meet the new boyfriend and he is sort of ugly, and I think to myself,
"Boy, my ex really downgraded."

The dreamer wouldn't know that his ex is in a new relationship unless he saw it on Facebook. Naturally, he wants to know what the person looks like, bringing up feelings of how he compares. His self-image might be rather low, because he doesn't put much time into getting ready for the big meeting, and in this dream "appearances" means the appearance we want people to see. I think his reaction upon meeting his dream's version of the new boyfriend—which has to be a projection of himself because he has never met or even seen the guy—shows something "ugly" about himself: the pettiness of comparing and ranking people based on their appearance and the feeling that maybe he doesn't measure up.

The ocean of information that fills the social media world is making us dream about people who have no meaning in our lives now. It is also making us aware of people in ways we might not want to, getting glimpses like never before into the daily lives of folks we don't really know. People who are plugged in all day say that their dreams are full of thoughts about stuff they read in their information feeds, like why their grade school teacher is now a transvestite, or the fact that their best friend from high school whom they haven't talked to in years "likes" PETA. At heart, what they are telling me is their dreams seem to have less personal significance when fragmented or full of miscellaneous trivia.

Technology has symbolic uses that dreams can use to tell stories. For instance, Facebook is appearing in dreams as a sort of town square, a place where we are seen in society, relationships are formed and maintained, and opinions are compared. Phones are used in dreams to beam messages directly from the unconscious mind, often as text messages. Email messages deliver information that move the dream story forward or reveal its meaning, or even reveal secrets. I've woken up knowing somehow that important email messages were waiting for me in my inbox. I have even experienced a few dreams when a voice spoke like an oracle from a cell phone.

Dreams process and filter a huge variety of experiences and feelings related to being plugged into a digital world. One theme that pops up a lot is approval from peers or recognition by society. This dream shows what I mean:

I find something under the skin of my index finger. I pull it out and realize that it is the Facebook Implant, which identifies who I am. I remove it and regret it later when my friends stop recognizing me.

The index finger is used to click a mouse button, so it is associated in this dream with the activity of using Facebook. Something about it has "gotten under his skin." It is the feeling that who he is as a person is defined through his life on Facebook, and that he wouldn't have friends or be recognized otherwise. This is really sad to think about, because those of us who have spent any time on Facebook know the jokes about who our friends really are compared to who our Facebook friends are.

In a dream expressing similar feelings, half of the dreamer's Facebook friends are suddenly blocked. I think this is a metaphor for Facebook friendships only being half of what a friendship can be. They have the regular contact and exchange of information of a "real" friendship, but no depth of feeling or relatedness. Here is another dream with that theme:

My parents take me to a hospital and I have a procedure done, and afterward I'm told something went wrong and I only have one day left to live; tomorrow I will fall into a permanent coma. So I go to update my Facebook status as: "brb, gotta die." Members of my extended family act like it is no big deal, and when they say goodbye it's like any other day, as if they don't care I'm about to go away forever. Simultaneously, like a storyline running underneath that the dream flashes to, my mom is dying and I'm in her bedroom with her for her last night alive. She asks me to put down my computer and spend some time with her, which I gladly do.

The hospital setting and the procedure symbolize that something in the dreamer is being worked on—but it's not physical; it's in his thoughts or feelings, and related to his parents. The second part of the dream points to the source: It's supposed to be his mom's last night alive (his, too) and how does he react? By fiddling on his computer, leaving pithy status updates. Dying in this dream means that something about their relationship is dying, and my sense is it's related to how much time he spends on a computer at the expense of deeper connection. That idea is reinforced by his extended family's reactions—"so long, have a nice trip"—when they know he is supposed to basically die the next day.

Going into a coma in this dream symbolizes the dreamer dying on the inside from the superficiality of his online life. He is eager for a deeper connection and deeper experience of life, shown in how he gladly puts down his computer to spend time with his mom. The procedure at the hospital symbolizes the need to live his life more fully, probably at the suggestion of his parents concerned by watching their son constantly preoccupied with a video screen. But what alternative is there, really, for someone in his situation? His social life is intrinsically connected with his life online, and to disconnect from it means social isolation.

Sleeping and dreaming are affected by technology in another way: For many people, their whiz-bang phones are with them constantly, within reach as they sleep, and those phones will beep and flash with activity all night long. Even if they don't, they still cast artificial light, and just a single LED light can interrupt the sleep cycle, which in turn interrupts dreaming. The effect can be as mild as a few missed dreams, or as severe as provoking sleep-walking, thrashing in bed, or a condition called sleep paralysis where the mind wakes up but the body is still asleep. Many hallucinations happening just after waking up can be explained by sleep paralysis.

Also, sleep cycles are messed up because people check their email and text messages at all hours. The constant interruption is having long-term consequences as we are increasingly sleep-deprived and unable to concentrate. As evidence accumulates, I think it might reveal more fragmentation in dreams caused by communication technology and social media. Perhaps in response the unconscious mind will throw out more metaphors and the sorts of pictures that say a thousand words. It will be interesting to see how we adapt.

Teeth

The most common part of the body featured in dreams, in my experience, is teeth: teeth falling out or being knocked out, missing teeth, ground-down teeth, broken teeth. The meaning is varied but usually comes down to one of four possibilities:

- You need to get your teeth checked. The dream is a literal warning or expression of fear.

- You have "lost face" in some way; your social status took a punch in the mouth.

- You feel powerless, ground down, unheard, or unable to express yourself verbally.

- You or someone you know has been lying, bragging, or stretching the truth.

Problems with teeth in dreams can indicate the need to see a dentist or take better care. It is a need that might not be consciously noticed at first because problems with teeth tend to develop slowly. For people who haven't seen a dentist in a long time, fear of dental problems can disturb their sleep.

Teeth are associated with social status and perceptions of attractiveness, so missing or broken teeth—especially front teeth—can be interpreted as loss of status or low self-image. In a dream discussed earlier, missing front teeth expresses the dreamer's fears that her new boyfriend does not meet her standards or the standards of her friends (page 173). A tooth falling out can symbolize "loss of face," or something spoken that lowers the person's social status. Losing a tooth is literally losing a part of your face!

Problems with teeth in dreams can also symbolize feeling frustrated at not being heard, difficulty expressing yourself, or the need to truly believe in what you say. For the same reason, loose teeth can be associated with loose speech, expressed in the old phrase "loose in the tooth." These days, liars and exaggerators are said to "play loose with truth." If, for example, you dream that you talk to a colleague and her tooth falls out while she speaks, it could be interpreted as you subconsciously know she lies, or that your opinion of her has dropped.

Work is sometimes called a "daily grind," and I've seen this idea symbolized by teeth ground down to describe situations that wear out a person. People who grind their teeth are often full of nervous tension.

Decayed teeth are associated with aging and fear of infirmity, or anything that can be described as rotting or decaying.

Two final thoughts about teeth in dreams: Teeth can be associated with change or transition, since growing in adult teeth is linked with transition out of childhood. It's a rite of passage which dreams can use in comparison to other rites of passage.

Also, teeth are sometimes taken for granted, and dreams can run with the idea and apply it to anything that is taken for granted, like health, safety, or relationships.

Video Games

Entire generations are growing up playing high-powered video games, many of which involve overcoming obstacles and conquering foes; and dreams draw on these themes frequently to tell stories about adventure, fantasy, conflict, and personal development. Perhaps in your dreams you are overcoming obstacles to your progress, or conquering anything standing in the way of reaching your goals the same way you might in a video game.

Video games are a terrific training ground for navigating the dream world, because in video games we learn to think through stressful or dangerous situations and solve problems imaginatively. Dr. Jayne Gackenbach found that people who regularly play video games are more likely to be able to control their dreams. For instance, if they find themselves chased by a monster in a dream, they might take control by teleporting the monster away, or growing swords for arms and battling it. Their gaming experience gives their imaginations more to work with, and even gives them the moxie to fight back. Controlling dreams raises the question of whether it is really the best idea, because dreams are the unconscious mind's opportunity to speak, but people who can take over their dreams report fewer nightmares. Perhaps to them, the monsters are just targets to blast.

If video games are a source of conflict, for instance, if the dreamer plays too much at the expense of other things, a dream about video games can symbolize this. The difference between those dreams and dreams about the adventure of personal development is seen in the action and the dreamer's feelings. If you dream you are your favorite video game hero winning battles and feeling good about it, you are probably dreaming about personal development or the adventures of life. If you dream you are trapped in a video game world and are struggling to get away, you might be spending too much time absorbed in the game.

Weapons

Weapons are reported frequently in dreams, often symbolizing expressions of anger, hurt feelings, or defensiveness. The setting, weapon, and opponent are all clues to help with the interpretation. I analyzed a dream where the weapon was a heavy fry pan, the setting a kitchen, and the opponent a ghoulish attacker chasing the dreamer around the house. We determined that the fry pan—a round object—represents the dreamer's ability to fight fear with holistic methods like deep breathing and centering. The kitchen is where ingredients come together to be cooked, and in dreams it is sometimes where we dream about new parts of ourselves combining or integrating. The dreamer hits her fears "head on" by whacking the attacker in the forehead with a fry pan to win the struggle and then helps him to his feet and has a long talk. The attacker turns out to be an avoided part of the dreamer trying to get her attention, and only looks ghoulish because she perceives him to be.

Weapons in dreams enact your feelings in graphic ways. The action of using a weapon indicates its connection to your daily life. Firing a weapon or using it against someone else can show defensiveness or anger directed outward. If a weapon is used against you or a character that symbolizes you, it represents anger directed, like in the dream about the boy cut in the stomach with a knife (page 121). And "weapons" used against us in daily life—for instance, old Facebook posts that come back to haunt, or things said in confidence that become public information—are sure to show up in dreams, sometimes as metaphors or figures of speech involving weapons or violence.

To help interpret the symbolism of weapons in your dreams, pay close attention to the actions and the area of the body that is affected. Use the list of body parts and what they can symbolize (page 143) as a reference.

Figures of speech use gun imagery like "staring down the barrel" or "under the gun" to describe stressful or dangerous situations, and so do dreams. In fact, analogies for guns, bullets, and shooting are riddled throughout the English language, giving the dreaming mind plenty to work with. Here is an example of a dream that describes a gun-related figure of speech. See if you can recognize it.

I'm at work, and all of my coworkers and I anxiously raise our heads above our cubicles to watch the elevator doors open, knowing it is the boss coming to our area to fire someone. The doors open and everyone ducks as a bullet buzzes over our heads, bounces off a door, and strikes the cubicle of the guy next to me. Luckily, he's out of the office.

The decision of the boss in this dream can be described as "fast as a bullet." The action of the bullet striking the cubicle next to the dreamer is an analogy for trouble that comes close but doesn't "impact" directly. Someone is said to "shoot" their chances or "get shot down" when they flub an audition, opportunity, or assignment, and dreams can easily run with that idea. Firing the gun symbolizes someone at the dreamer's work about to be fired.

Firing a gun at someone in a dream is a raw way of expressing how you feel about that person or what he or she represents, loud and direct, or of identifying them as a source of conflict. A silenced gun, on the other hand, can show that feelings are not being expressed—they are "silenced," not allowed full expression. A gun fired at you during a dream can symbolize what it feels like to be on the receiving end of someone's anger—including anger at yourself. When anger is bottled up or ineffective, the gun will jam, or fire Nerf balls, for example, instead of bullets. Childish anger can be represented by toy guns.

Gun owners who frequently think about or use their weapons are likely to dream about them to describe how it feels and what it represents in their lives. A gun can make the owner feel safer or give a false sense of confidence. People who carry guns for a living have more to consider when dreaming about them; for instance, a police officer or soldier who dreams that a gun jams might feel that his or her career progress is jammed. A dream of a gun that accidentally fires can symbolize directing anger at the wrong person, "misfiring" a bad idea or plan, having an explosive temper touched off at the slightest provocation—a "hair trigger."

In one of my dreams, a gun represents the desire to right wrongs. Here is the relevant scene:

From inside my house I look out the front door and see a man in my yard armed with two holstered pistols on his hips. I feel uneasy and threatened with his presence near my home.

The two guns grab my attention. Who is the man carrying them outside my home? Since I'm under no outside threats and the literal interpretation doesn't fit, I ask if he is a part of myself: a perception, an attitude, a feeling. Then I remember a small incident that made a big impression on me as a teenager when I met a martial arts master who transported prisoners and carried duel pistols for his job. He was the kind of guy who didn't have to take shit from anyone and didn't feel the need to prove it. In my mind he turned into a sort of "Equalizer" figure, someone who fought against the wrongs of the world.

The day before the dream, I watched a news report about a cop who turned off his dash cam and beat an old man with dementia, but a backup camera recorded the heartless savagery. It really made my blood boil, and I had a daydream of being in the scene to stop the beating. In the daydream I carried two pistols in holsters, just like the threatening presence outside my home. Connection made, I realize that the man in the dream symbolizes the part of myself that wants to right the wrongs of the world at the point of a gun. He would impose my sense of justice.

Like guns and shooting, knives and cutting have a lot of potential symbolic uses, seen in figures of speech like "knife in the back" to describe betrayal and "sharp as a knife" to describe incisive thinking. Any reference to knifing or cutting in a dream should first be taken as a possible warning to be more careful with sharp objects; the dream coach might have observed danger signs. If you work with knives for a living and dream of injuring yourself with one (or any object while doing any job or activity, for that matter), be especially careful! Dreams can be literal, and one of their primary functions is self-preservation.

If not a literal warning, consider the symbolic interpretations and focus on the action with the knife. Knives are used for protection and can symbolize keeping something or someone at a distance, which can also be said for guns. They can be used to take control of a situation, or to imply a lack of power or authority. They can represent the need for sharp or tough decision making. They can be used to cut something off or remove something surgically. Dreams about cutting off body parts can express the need to remove something from your life, or perhaps to sever ties. If the blade is prominent in the dream it might be a metaphor for "razor's edge."

For a terrific example of knife symbolism, see "Skinless Creature Wants My Skin," coming up next.

The Final Step: Putting It All Together

In this final section we will look at dreams that bring together everything I've shown you. I hope you can identify a lot of what is happening in these dreams before I explain them. They are pretty long and complex, and if you are stumped don't be disheartened! Being able to discuss these dreams with the dreamers over the course of weeks and sometimes months lends an incredible amount of insight into the interpretation that can't be gained from just reading a summary.

Skinless Creature Wants My Skin

I'm folding laundry in my bedroom when I hear a noise downstairs. I peer down and see a human-shaped creature with no skin—the muscles, tendons, and arteries are exposed and wet—carrying a big knife. It wants to take my skin as a disguise so it can hide inside and do terrible things. When it sees me, it dashes up the steps.

I run into the bathroom and grab Epsom salts. The phrase "salt in an open wound" comes to mind. I throw salt onto the exposed flesh of the creature. It screams in pain. I run, but realize I didn't take away its knife.

It chases me outside and we fight in the middle of the street. The creature cuts me deeply on the arm. I push it away and a city bus smashes into it and blood flies everywhere. Two men grab me, thinking I've harmed an innocent bystander, despite the creature's hideous face clearly showing. It starts to get up.

This dream opens with a clue to its meaning found in the action: Folding laundry can describe straightening up one's life, taking care of business, keeping up appearances. The bedroom setting is a clue that the dream is about something in the dreamer's thoughts related to her overall life—she is pondering, reflecting back. The bathroom setting suggests that the dream is also about appearances, public persona, or cleaning up something, such as an unresolved situation. The creature's knife characterizes the nature of the dreamer's conflict and her feeling about the underlying situation: It cuts like a knife.

The creature wants her skin to disguise itself. Since skin is associated with persona, something trying to take the dreamer's skin can be related to identity theft or revenge tactics that strike at a person's reputation. It could symbolize that she has been falsely portrayed. (You will see in a moment how that interpretation fits the dream; right now I'm walking you through how I interpreted it by considering all possibilities.)

I think the creature itself symbolizes what the dreamer feels like: a raw wound. One sign that the skinless creature represents a wounded side of the dreamer is found in the phrase she thinks of during the dream: "salt in an open wound." It is definitely meaningful because it arises spontaneously and symbolically acts out how she feels. Often in dreams featuring conflict and struggle, the thing you fight is actually yourself, but it can also symbolize an outside force. Either way, the dream character is a projection of the dreamer.

The cut to the dreamer's arm while fighting in the street with the creature appears to symbolize harm to the dreamer's work life, since arms and hands are what we use to carry out most work tasks. Two men grab the dreamer in the end like she is responsible, instead of seeing and grabbing the creature, which suggests she feels like she has been falsely accused of something. If she had accepted the blame in the dream, it would indicate that she knows deep inside she has brought her trouble on herself.

After I offer an initial interpretation of the dream, the dreamer relates to the part about conflict. At the time of the dream, she was involved in a legal battle with a former employer over a workplace injury, so the wound to the arm makes sense when seen as a symbolic wounding to her work life. She said her employer retaliated after she filed a complaint while still on the job, and that her former supervisor tried to sabotage her new work situation. In this sense the former work situation "stalks" her like the creature, and salt in the wound is a good way of summing up how the dreamer felt about it. The gist of the dream can be figured out just by asking the dreamer, "How do you relate to the feeling of salt in an open wound?"

Because a formal complaint is involved, the city bus represents a public dispute, and the two men who grab the dreamer represent her feelings that she was unfairly blamed by the former employer for getting hurt on the job. Her personal information ties the details of the dream together: the skinless creature, the stalking, the knife, the wound to the arm, the conflict. Except for one little detail: The dreamer has been dreaming about the creature since she was a young child. The feeling of something wanting her skin had pursued her for a long time.

Even though the dreamer appears to have been wrongly treated by an employer, it's possible that she has a pattern of sabotaging herself, represented as the creature. If so, it will become obvious through conversations with it. I suggested the dreamer try using her imagination to relate the creature to her life and feelings. Ultimately, victory over whatever it symbolizes will occur when the dreamer fully embraces the creature and accepts it as part of herself.

Playing Guitar in a Hotel Lobby

I'm older than I am now, in a hotel lobby, and a bored employee watches over musical instruments that belong to a famous rock group that stayed at the hotel the night before. There is a beautiful guitar, and even though I don't know how to play it I ask the employee if I can try. "You should," he replies. So I pick up the guitar and begin playing exactly what I feel inside, and it comes out perfectly.

I close my eyes and somehow the guitar becomes my teenage daughter, even though I don't really have a daughter. She and the guitar are one, and her shirt is the same blue color as the guitar. She tells me she is sorry she died—it wasn't suicide, but she was responsible for her own death. I tell her it's alright, and that she didn't know it but she was pregnant when she died and would have made a wonderful mother.

Finally, my fingers are too sore to play anymore, and I put the guitar back after a tearful goodbye to my daughter, telling the hotel employee that there is something special about the guitar. He replies, "It's the player who makes it special."

What a dream! To begin interpreting it, start with the hotel setting. It is used most often to describe a place of transition, and I think it describes transition in the dreamer's perceptions of himself. The action of playing out his feelings through an instrument he has never touched—an instrument that "belongs" to a famous rock band—is related to the dreamer's perceptions of himself as a creative person. He has feelings to express and innately knows how to do it through his creativity, shown in the action of playing an instrument he has never played before. The reference to the famous rock band probably means he is innately talented, and music is an art form closely associated with emotion and feeling.

Since a child is a creation, the unborn daughter symbolizes the creativity the dreamer doesn't use. As if the action of playing a guitar that morphs into his daughter is not enough of a clue, the dream makes another connection: The color of her shirt matches the guitar, and blue is associated with thought and feeling. She might symbolize how the dreamer's artistic side reached a "teen-age" stage of development before it receded. It wasn't suicide—he didn't "kill off" his artistic side—but he is somehow responsible because he didn't use it. Maybe he didn't value it enough in him-self at the time; perhaps he had other priorities. The reference to the daughter being pregnant when she died symbolizes that the dreamer was at one time "pregnant" with creativity.

The dreamer's progressed age in the dream, I think, is predict-ing his future as someone who could have used his talent more but didn't. During the interpretation he relates to the idea of his daughter being a symbol for unused artistic talent. His job as a video editor is inherently creative, but time constraints prevent him from putting any feeling or extra touches into it. The hotel employee character is bored, and that is how the dreamer feels about his work.

The interpretation's clincher comes from the employee's two statements. When the dreamer asks if he can play the guitar, the employee says, "You should." And when the dreamer puts the guitar down and comments that there is something spe-cial about it, the employee replies, "It's the player who makes it special." The first statement is a message from the unconscious mind that the dreamer should express his feelings through cre-ativity; he has talent and passion. The unconscious is the source of creativity, and has wise things to say about its use. The second statement confirms that it doesn't matter what creative outlets he chooses, the dreamer adds the magic. He makes whatever he creates special.

The resolution of the dream is for the dreamer to use his cre-ative talents before the opportunity is gone. While the dreamer is sad about what is lost, his dream shows him it is not too late. It would not give him this poignant message unless he could do something constructive with the information.

My Boyfriend the Murderer

There is a car crash and a family of five dies. It is investigated as a homicide after a young girl in the car is found with her mouth sewn shut. Because of a playing card found at the scene that came from my boyfriend's deck, I suspect he is the killer. I'm afraid he'll find out I know what he did, but I'm staying in the same apartment with him. Later I take a shower and the shower head turns into my boyfriend's face. I freak out and yell at him to go away.

The first big clue to the meaning of this dream is the car crash. Traveling together in a car can symbolize a relationship, in this case, the dreamer's family relationship. Even though a different family is portrayed in the dream, it's really her family relationship the dream addresses—the generic family is used as a surrogate. Their death in the dream suggests that the dreamer's family life is facing a big change or transition, which turns out to be the case: At the time of the dream she is preparing to leave home and move in with her boyfriend.

Next the dream gives a clue that connects her boyfriend (and what he represents) with the murdered family: the playing card. Cards can be used to predict the future, and this dream is predicting the future of the dreamer's relationship with her family if she moves in with her boyfriend. She is having doubts about the move, shown in her reaction of fearing that her boyfriend will find out that she suspects he is responsible for murdering the family in the dream, but she is afraid of voicing them.

I think the young girl with her mouth sewn shut shows how the dreamer's fear prevents her from voicing her doubts. Fear figuratively sews shut her mouth, and the girl character probably symbolizes the formative time of life when she learned not to voice doubts or take action when needed. Or, perhaps it shows she is somehow being childish. Either way, the child is used by the dream as a surrogate for the dreamer.

The apartment setting symbolizes the dreamer's transition away from living with her family, and the fact that she already lives with her boyfriend in the dream identifies her relationship with him as part of that transition. It's also a glimpse of a possible future with less privacy, symbolized when the shower head turns into her boyfriend's face.

The action of showering suggests that the dreamer needs to cleanse herself of something. It could be nervousness, doubt, or fear. On the other hand, it could be the boyfriend she needs to cleanse herself of; I had to wonder how well she really knew him.

Her reaction of freaking out is a clue that she knows something is wrong about the relationship or herself. She could have reacted to the presence of her boyfriend in the shower by saying, "Hey, if the rest of you is in that pipe, why don't you pop out and join me?" but she didn't. Generally, the bigger the freak out, the stronger the feelings behind it.

The resolution of the dream is to think through the implications of moving in with her boyfriend, with the knowledge that it's probably a bad idea, either because he is not the right guy, or she is not ready to make the transition to being on her own. The real key to this dream is it is predicting the future; the dreamer still has time to avoid making a bad mistake. Even if the boyfriend is a great guy in waking life, the dreamer is obviously not ready to live with him. Her feelings are too conflicted, and the dream tries very hard to make her aware of what is going on beneath the surface of her thoughts and feelings.

There is another clue I did not mention because you would have to know something about numerology to recognize it: the family of five. The dreamer is from a family of four, so the discrepancy stands out as intentional. The number five in dreams is a sign of impending change, according to Edgar Cayce, and in this dream it couldn't be more true. The number five has other numerological meanings, but in this case the interpretation of impending change fits the dreamer's current situation. If you'd like to know more about numerology and the dream interpretations of Edgar Cayce, *Dreams: Your Magic Mirror* by Elsie Sechrist is an excellent place to start.

Disappearing White Figure at the Front Door

I come home from school and my grandpa is waiting in a car in the driveway. He says my family has moved and he is supposed to drive me to my new home. We drive there and the house is a lot like the old one, except there is a ladder instead of steps at the front entrance. My family and neighbors are inside having a housewarming party, but I don't join in; instead I look around—which gets difficult as more people enter and the house becomes crowded. Eventually they all leave and I'm left alone.

I sit down in a chair with a view of the front door and notice a white figure on the other side of the glass looking through it. The glass is frosted so I can't see the figure clearly. I open the door and the figure vanishes before I get a good look. I sit down again and peer toward the door, and see the figure run full speed into the glass, leaving the imprints of two hands, but when I open the door no one is there. The next time it appears I see it coming and run to the door ready to punch someone, but again no one is there.

Finally I leave the door open and wait. I see the figure coming again, but when I get up, it backs away so I don't get a clear look. I lock the door and go back to my chair. The figure is outside the door again like it never left. I close the curtains and turn off the lights. It starts knocking.

Moving into a new home implies starting a new phase of life, and the first sign that it will be a more solitary life is the ladder to enter the home. Ladders can only be traversed one person at a time. The next sign is the dreamer's reaction to his family's presence by staying apart, followed by the scene of the house crowded with people. It says to me that he prefers his solitude, and the presence of a lot of people in his life blocks his "view" of who he is inside, a sign of introversion. Then he is left alone to begin his new life, and the action begins at the front door.

A home in a dream often symbolizes the dreamer, and the front door is where people enter a home, so the front door can represent the line between the dreamer's personal and public life. The frosted glass symbolizes that the dreamer's future as a solitary person has not yet become clear to him, but he senses it coming. The symbolism is reinforced by the chair, which only fits one person at a time. I suspect that he prefers to be alone but fears complete isolation.

When dream characters are indistinct, like the white figure, I ask if they symbolize feelings or perceptions about an overall topic. It is not a specific person at the front door; it's not anyone at all, as the dreamer finds out repeatedly when he opens the door and finds no one there. It is the fear of isolation that pesters him to the point of wanting to punch someone, and its persistence shows it isn't going away.

The handprints on the glass remind me of someone alone looking out a window; it is the dreamer's view of life as an introvert looking out. The handprints are on the outside of the glass, which might say "outside looking in," but in this dream it describes a situation of the dreamer being inside of himself (his house) looking out. The dreamer is, in a sense, observing himself in the action with the white figure.

The presence of the dreamer's grandfather in the dream ties it all together, because he is an introvert, too, and the dreamer sees himself in his grandfather, content to sit in a chair and watch the world go round. The new phase of life the dreamer is entering, symbolized by moving into a new house, reminds him of what his grandpa's life is like, so in the dream his grandpa drives him there. I see it as a way of saying, "You are like me, and that is alright." It's fine to be introverted, this dreamer just needs to resolve some issues about the boundaries he sets between his public and private life.

The next dream we look at can be confused for separate dreams, but it is really one long story. The dreamer even woke to use the bathroom, went back to sleep, and the dream continued seemingly throughout the night. It is a great dream for illustrating how several seemingly disconnected dreams tell one story and are used to verify the interpretation.

Mafia Slave

Act 1: *I go to a hotel that looks like a Victorian house outside. Behind the front desk is an older woman with gray hair dyed platinum blonde, and a man around her age is nearby in the mailroom. I'm seven years old and on my own, an orphan. I check in.*

Act 2: *I'm a teenager stealing makeup in a department store. I think I'm going to get caught so I head to the changing rooms for women. The female attendant says I'm not allowed in because I look like a boy.*

Act 3: *I'm college age and with two FBI agents in a square courtyard, looking for a door. I see the door, which is hidden to the side. I debate whether I should tell them, but end up pointing it out. Inside is a group of Mafia guys led by a tall, older man. They capture me. I tell the leader I wasn't trying to betray him to the agents even though I really was. I am afraid he will kill me.*

Act 4: *I'm older now and the Mafia leader wants to marry me off. I poison the suitor with white powder in his food that dissolves his heart. He is taken away to the hospital and comes back with an artificial heart. I pretend like I didn't do it, but the tall Mafia leader suspects me. They go forward with the wedding, now to a different guy, a sadist. My mom is there. The wedding dress makes my breasts off-kilter, and I'm self-conscious.*

Act 5: *I'm the slave of the sadistic Mafia guy. He handcuffs me to a bed in a one-room, dimly lit apartment and forces me to make him meals, leaving the leftovers on the plates to attract ants. The ants cover my face and bite me, causing my skin to swell and pockmark. I look hideous. The sadist leaves me handcuffed in the apartment while he is gone. Two women who look like Charlie's Angels come to the door looking for something and break in to free me. Then they go through his stuff and find a black handgun. The sadist returns and we struggle for the gun. I end up with it and point it at him. To prove I'll use it, I fire next to his head, and the bullet bounces around the room.*

Act 6: *I return to the hotel at my present age. There is a message from my father. It says, "If I'd known you needed me like you did while you were growing up, I would have been there for you." There is also a thick envelope from my mother, but I wake up before having the chance to open it.*

Despite being broken into what could be understood as separate dreams, there is a continuous story here of a girl confronted with complicated issues at a young age, seen in Act 1. The Victorian house symbolizes the dreamer's life as viewed from her unconscious mind. The older woman at the counter represents her mother, who has platinum blonde hair, and the man in the mailroom represents her father—"mailroom" actually meaning "male room." The dreamer checks in to the hotel as a seven-year-old orphan, symbolizing how her family life transitioned at that age and she faced many challenges alone because her father was away a lot on business—not technically an orphan, but it felt that way. Those challenges continue into adulthood, so the dream takes her back in time to when it all began, providing an opportunity to understand and heal.

The story moves forward in Act 2 as the girl confronts puberty on her own. She "steals" makeup, meaning she learned about and wore makeup against her mother's wishes. The dreamer told me that as a result, as an early teenager she dressed in baggy clothes and cut off her long hair to avoid being noticed by boys, symbolized in the dream when the dressing room attendant turns her away because she looks like a boy.

In Act 3 the dream progresses to show the dreamer an older version of herself that has developed a complex—an area of the psyche "gone rogue"—symbolized by the tall Mafia guy. His henchmen symbolize other parts of the dreamer's psyche recruited to work against her. Mafia implies family, and her family life is a subject of this dream. The FBI agents are there to lead her to the source of the problem. The unconscious mind is aware of what is going on even if the conscious mind isn't, and it uses dream figures like agents and detectives to pass along clues that lead the dreamer in the right direction.

The dreamer is presented with a choice at this stage: point out the door for the agents or pretend not to notice. Her reaction shows she is willing to confront the complex, though she is scared and still under its influence. She could have pretended she didn't see the door, but she decides to go forward because even though the situation appears dangerous, she subconsciously knows it is to her benefit to investigate the situation. The square configuration with the door hidden on one side tipped me off that an archetype was at work, which I later identified as the shadow side of the Warrior.

Act 4 starts to get to the root of the complex produced by the anxiety and uncertainty of the dreamer's formative years. The marriage in the dream symbolizes psychological bonding with the complex—her ego has come under its power, controlling her with fear. Her reaction by poisoning the suitor shows where the complex took root: in her feelings, her heart. Dissolving the heart with poison shows how the dreamer tries to shut down her feelings by poisoning them with toxic thoughts, but the suitor comes back with an artificial heart, symbolizing that feelings of self-esteem were replaced with a poor substitute. Replacing the first suitor with a sadist is the dream's way of showing the evolution of the complex. It began as her poisoning herself in a sense, and results in marriage to a sadist. Sadomasochism arises from the Warrior archetype's shadow side.

The awkward fit of the wedding dress has two layers of meaning: One, the marriage does not "fit" her, and two, the dreamer's breasts make her feel awkward. The feeling has its roots in Act 2 when the teenager doesn't learn what she needs to know about her gender. It gives the complex ammunition to attack her self-image.

The enslavement to the sadistic dream character in Act 5 is an illustration of the dreamer's relationship to the complex, like slave to master or masochist to sadist. The complex must be "fed" like a parasite, and the dreamer prepares its meals. What does it feed on? Her feelings, represented in the dream as ants that cover and bite her face. Each bite is a thought that crosses her mind when she looks in the mirror, and the voice of the complex speaks in her head, biting into her feelings. The grotesque, swollen face she sees in the dream symbolizes her fear that something is wrong with her appearance, which the sadist has convinced her of and uses to keep her internally handcuffed, once again pointing back to Act 2 when the young teenager was denied the opportunity to learn how to use makeup and handle her physical change from girl to woman.

Next, the dream points to a resolution when the two women show up to help the dreamer. The pair represents her potential to feel attractive in a way that is balanced and healthy, showing her a different image of herself. With it she can free herself from the complex, which challenges her when it returns to the dream scene. She fires the gun in self-defense, showing she is ready to stand up for herself, but the bouncing bullet is a perfect metaphor for how anger can backfire. When she aims near the sadist's head and fires, she points out where the complex lives: in her head.

The dreamer must ultimately remember that she is dealing with herself, not a Mafia boss and his henchmen, and as much as she'd like to kill the complex, she'd kill off a part of herself in the process. Behind the woman enslaved in the drab apartment is a little girl who found herself on her own at a young age and did her best to survive, and that little girl is trying to find her way home. Gentleness and understanding are required.

In Act 6 the dream resolves when the dreamer returns to the hotel and has a message waiting from her father. Here the connection is made between him and the man in the mailroom. The message that he would have been there for her if he had known she needed him is exactly what she needs to know to move on. As a young girl she missed him terribly when he was away on business, and even wondered if something was wrong with her to make him leave town. That seed of self-doubt eventually grew into a complex.

Act 6 verifies the interpretation of Act 1 as the opening of a story about the dreamer's life, beginning with a formative event of her childhood, and ending with gaining what was needed back then to help her grow up with a healthy image of herself. It verifies that the six acts are interrelated and tell one story. The thick envelope from her mother is a sign of things to come, when she works through the same process of healing the past with her. The resolution of the dream is to take the information gained and use it to free herself.

The next couple of dreams are about the shadow side of the mind we talked about earlier in the dream characters section (see page 38).

Baby Draws Unbelievable Pictures

I'm in a hotel ballroom along with my wife, and everyone is there to celebrate the birth of my child, though in waking life I have neither a wife nor a child. The child isn't even a month old and it can draw. Not squiggles and random figures you would expect from a baby— discernible pictures. I know it's not right, but everyone else thinks it's a sign of intelligence or something cute. A big black guy the size of Mike Tyson is there with me. I tell him it's abnormal for a child that age to draw so well. The child draws a crazy-looking happy face on my wrist, then says to me, "Your blood will rain" and cuts three straight lines below the happy face. I wake up scared shitless.

The ballroom setting announces the dream as a story about the dreamer's relationship with society. Young people used to be introduced to the public at society balls. We see the idea at work when the baby cuts the lines in the dreamer's wrist, interpreted as meaning the dreamer will have three children who will continue his "blood line." There is also a premonition in the baby's statement, "Your blood will rain." I think what it really means is "your blood will *reign*," as in rule or lead. (Dreams famously use wordplay like this.) The baby is shown to the public in the ballroom, and my sense is that it represents how the dreamer will eventually take his place in society as a father. But the dreamer's reaction to the baby's drawing shows that something about the "picture" of himself in that role causes internal resistance when, like the happy face, it should bring him joy.

The Mike Tyson character he appeals to shows the source of the resistance in his shadow side—it could be that the dreamer can't see himself as a father yet; he is still living the bachelor life, and the thought of having children is "crazy." Fatherhood is a scary thought for a young man still discovering himself. The dream shows he is freaked out by it, but the marks on his wrist indicate it is predetermined, part of his destiny. The wrist is the connector to the hand, so in dreams a mark or bite on the wrist can signify things that need to be done, because hands are used to take action. However, the dreamer can choose a different destiny and the blood lines will disappear. The future shown to him is a possibility that will become reality only if he chooses it.

The Tyson character also depicts the nature of his personal shadow, which takes on distinct characteristics depending on the person. I think that in this case a black-skinned man was chosen to represent the dreamer's shadow side because of the association with the person of Mike Tyson, but it could very well have arisen from the dreamer's personal experience. The muscular, tough guy image is the opposite of the dream's vision of the dreamer as a caring father, and probably illustrates the attitude behind the dreamer's resistance to the message of the dream: The dreamer's shadow side would rather live without any restrictions or rules like Tyson, who at one time was completely out of control. The comparison is exaggerated but fitting.

Getting Away with Murder at Laura's House

I wander into the house of Laura Linney's character from the movie Love Actually. *She's not happy to have me there because I interrupt her and her guests from watching a movie. I end up falling asleep in a guest bedroom and wake up to my masterpiece: four dead bodies on the bed arranged in a cross, blood everywhere. A voice in my head says that anal sex is somehow involved. So I run away, but the neighbors are watching; they've seen my face on signs warning about me. A neighbor tries to stop me in the garden. Then I see this black guy across a field and wave to him and say something cool. He waves back and points me toward a door in the fence. I go through it and get away free!*

Blonde, poised, and attractive, Laura Linney embodies the classic image of the anima, and the movie *Love Actually* is about love and relationships. So I interpret the opening of this dream as a story about the dreamer's experience with, or feelings about, love and relationships. He interrupts the scene at the beginning and isn't wanted, the first hint that something's not right. Anima rejects an ego that indulges in darkness or stupidity, the same as most women will.

The scene in the bed is the next clue that points to something twisted. The arrangement of four bloody bodies as a cross implies the death of something in the psyche. On the other hand, it also could be an unconscious plea for help, as in "red cross." Anal sex for some people is another way of saying "took it up the ass," which probably symbolizes how the dreamer feels about his love life or life in general: like he is being screwed in a way that is not at all enjoyable (the symbolism could mean something completely different to someone who enjoys anal sex). Yet it is also his "masterpiece," and in my mind, only an ego influenced by shadow would view such a scene that way. He sees the mess he has created of himself and is proud of it.

Connecting the scene with the opening of the dream, I wonder if the dreamer has been through trauma in his love life that turned him cold. To fill the void left by loss, or lack, of love, we can bitterly turn against it to protect ourselves against pain or disappointment. The bed is a place where a person dreams, and "dreams" in another sense mean hopes and aspirations. So by the implied actions that happen in the bed, I see someone who turns against himself and "murders" his hopes and aspirations.

Anima can't inspire a man with no hope. Sleeping in a dream can be a way of saying that something happens unconsciously—the dreamer is driven by forces inside of himself that he is not consciously aware of; he is sleeping through life.

The dreamer's reaction of running away shows that he knows at some level he has been doing something harmful to himself, and the neighbors watching out for him indicate that his unconscious mind views him as a danger to himself. Then, finally, his shadow appears.

The black-skinned man across the field, a representation of the dreamer's shadow side, is behind everything to this point in the dream. He symbolizes the inner voice that leads the dreamer astray, the voice that convinces him that waking up next to four dead bodies is somehow cool. He identifies with his shadow when he waves like they are buddies and it shows him a getaway route. That's not to say that black-skinned dream characters are always representatives of your shadow side, only that black as a color is closely connected with the unknown, and shadow is the unknown parts of yourself.

Sometimes it's easiest to interpret a dream by starting at the end and working backwards. In this dream, this final clue that the dreamer might be strongly influenced, or even taken over, by his shadow ties together the rest of the dream. Shadow will try to make the dreamer believe it is his friend, the one person he can trust, when in reality its agenda is to take over as much of a person as it can.

The getaway route is symbolic of how the shadow offers justifications to make the conscience feel better, an escape from feelings of guilt, or from second thoughts—but in doing so the dreamer follows the direction of his shadow. Leaving the garden, combined with the cross of dead bodies in the previous scene, looks to me like a metaphor for a fallen state of being—like when

Adam and Eve were tossed out of the Garden of Eden. I can't say for sure because the dreamer didn't respond to my interpretation.

Tip

Shadow can reveal truths hidden from you, but everything it reveals comes with a price. The best way to handle your shadow is to pay attention—but don't listen too closely. Don't let it get to your feelings. Shine the light of self-awareness into every dark corner of your being to take away its hiding places. Assume that every truth it tells you comes with a lie or two.

Dance of My Soul

I'm seated in a packed theater watching a fantastic sort of dance on stage. To gain a better view, I use a telescoping lens, the old-style long brass tube, and see that the dancers move elegantly in a clockwise circle. I'm reminded of Cirque du Soleil by the flow and coordination of the dance, and by the dancers' outfits, feathery and light. What I see is like a living kaleidoscope, shapes and colors emerging from and receding into the rotating center.

This is one of my most powerful dreams, and I learned gradually that represented in it is the dance of my innermost being. The telescoping lens, an elongated circle, provides a view of this inner process, showing me that beneath my life among the audience of humanity is an interior life of beauty and grace. That innermost life in the center of my being is separate from my outer life, seen from a distance like in the dream, yet from it emerges everything. Every new combination of my interior parts is put together by a kaleidoscopic dance in my center, my soul. Even the association with Cirque du Soleil, which means "Circle of the Sun," ties together the idea, because the sun is the center of the solar system and gives life. Pretty cool dream, eh?

✳✳✳

Before concluding, let's sum up the three steps of *Dreams 1-2-3*:

1. Recognize the importance of your dreams and remember them. Write them down. Learn their structure, symbolism, and storytelling qualities.

2. Discover the meaning of your dreams by associating the details with your life, whether your inner life or your outer life. Pay close attention to your feelings, and remember that almost everything is symbolic. Speak the language and decipher the messages.

3. Live your dreams by making them part of your daily life and following where they lead. Work with your dreams while awake, realizing they are products of your imagination. Use your dreams to create your future.

Following these steps will get you started on a lifetime journey of self-discovery with dreams as your guide. Go where they lead and you are assured it is the right direction, and you will enjoy the ride. Everything you need to reach your destination is inside you. Just close your eyes and pay attention. Happy dreaming.

Conclusion

I can't guarantee that every interpretation here is 100 percent accurate. Many of the dreams I use in this book are from Internet posts, and while I picked mostly from interpretations that the dreamers affirmed, some dreamers didn't respond. However, a portion of the dreams are my own or from people close to me, and I am as sure about the interpretations as I can be. Some of my dreams took years to fully decipher, and I'm confident of the interpretations because they were confirmed by subsequent dreams and events.

Also, most of the dream descriptions are condensed for readability.

A maddening fact of dream interpretation is its subjectivity, so rather than obsess with always being right, I focus instead on teaching the process. Once you wrap your mind around it, dream interpretation is intuitive, natural. Everyone dreams, therefore, everyone is a dream interpreter. As I've said before, you are the author of your dreams, and you know what the stories mean. A dream interpreter reminds you of what you already know. You can do that for yourself with the help of your dreams.

I would also like to note that while dream interpretation is aided by knowledge of psychology, it's not at all necessary. I'm no psychologist; I studied government and journalism in college. Dream interpretation used to be a family and community tradition, and it goes back thousands if not tens of thousands of years. It should be common knowledge and can be again with the right voices explaining it.

If you would like to share your dreams and get to know a great community of dream enthusiasts, drop by the Reddit dream forum listed in my bio. I'm known there as RadOwl.

Peace,

Jason M. DeBord

P.S. If you like what you have read, I could use your help spreading the word. Your review of this book on Amazon or Goodreads makes it more likely my work will be noticed. Every mention on social media or otherwise is greatly appreciated. Thank you!

Bibliography

Faraday, Ann. *The Dream Game.* New York: Harper & Row, 1974.

Johnson, Robert A. *Inner Work: Using Dreams and Active Imagination for Personal Growth.* New York: Harper & Row, 1989.

———. *Owning Your Own Shadow: Understanding the Dark Side of the Psyche.* San Francisco: Harper & Row, 1993.

Jung, C. G., et al. *Man and His Symbols.* New York: Dell, 1968.

Moore, Robert, and Douglas Gillette. *King, Magician, Warrior, Lover: Rediscovering the Archetypes of the Mature Masculine.* New York: HarperOne, 1991.

Pesavento, Larry. *Toward Manhood: Into the Wilderness of the Soul.* Cincinnati: Larry Pesavento, 2010. Available on Kindle.

Sechrist, Elsie. *Dreams: Your Magic Mirror.* New York: Cowles Education Corporation, 1968.

About the Author

Hawke Taylore

J. M. DeBord has worked in publishing for twenty-five years. He is the author of *The Third King: A New Age Thriller*, a novel about the Second Coming of a completely unexpected messiah. He maintains a blog about dreams at *http://dreams123.net* and a collection of other writing at *http://groovywriter.com*. He also has a website devoted to this book and its teachings, *Dreams1-2-3.com*. You can find him on Facebook at *www.facebook.com/interpretdreams* and on Reddit's dream forum at *www.reddit.com/r/dreams*, where he is a moderator. He lives in Tucson, Arizona.

Hampton Roads Publishing Company
. . . for the evolving human spirit

Hampton Roads Publishing Company
publishes books on a variety of subjects,
including spirituality, health,
and other related topics.

For a copy of our latest trade catalog,
call (978) 465-0504 or visit our distributor's website
at *www.redwheelweiser.com.*
You can also sign up for our newsletter
and special offers by going to
www.redwheelweiser.com/newsletter.